13
Proven Ways to Get Your Message Across

CORWIN
PRESS

The Corwin Press logo — a raven striding across an open book — represents the happy union of courage and learning. We are a professional-level publisher of books and journals for K–12 educators, and we are committed to creating and providing resources that embody these qualities. Corwin's motto is "Success for All Learners."

13 Proven Ways to Get Your Message Across

The Essential Reference for Teachers, Trainers, Presenters, and Speakers

Ernest W. Brewer

CORWIN PRESS, INC.
A Sage Publications Company
Thousand Oaks, California

For information:

Corwin Press, Inc.
A Sage Publications Company
2455 Teller Road
Thousand Oaks, California 91320
E-mail: order@corwin.sagepub.com

SAGE Publications Ltd.
6 Bonhill Street
London EC2A 4PU
United Kingdom

SAGE Publications India Pvt. Ltd.
M-32 Market
Greater Kailash I
New Delhi 110 048 India

Printed in the United States of America

Library of Congress Cataloging-in-Publication Data

Brewer, Ernest W.
    13 proven ways to get your message across / Ernest W. Brewer.
        p.   cm.
    Includes bibliographical references.
    ISBN 0-8039-6641-5 (cloth : alk. paper).—ISBN
0-8039-6642-3 (pbk. : alk. paper)
    1. Teaching.   2. Teachers—Training of.   3. Teacher
effectiveness.   I. Title.
    LB1027.B747   1997
    370'.711—dc21   97-22291

This book is printed on acid-free paper.

97 98 99 00 01 02 10 9 8 7 6 5 4 3 2 1

Production Editor: S. Marlene Head
Editorial Assistant: Kristen L. Gibson
Cover Designer: Marcia R. Finlayson

Contents

About the Author

Ernest W. Brewer is Associate Professor and Principal Investigator/ Project Director in the Department of Human Resource Development, College of Human Ecology, The University of Tennessee, Knoxville. His primary focus is teaching graduate courses, conducting workshops, advising graduate students, serving on graduate student committees, and administering seven funded projects. These funded projects mainly serve economically disadvantaged youth and adults, U. S. military veterans, school dropouts, stopouts, displaced workers, individuals with handicaps, minorities, and women under-represented in math and science fields. His administrative activities require overseeing 45-55 full- and part-time professionals and support staff who serve these individuals. Serving as the Principal Investigator/Director of multiple funded projects, he supervises and works with a variety of graduate students that he employs as instructors, counselors, and/or tutors on the funded projects that he administers. Prior to joining the university in 1976, he earned his doctorate degree in Technological and Adult Education and served as the Executive Director of the Institute of Human Resources.

Over the last 19 years he has acquired external funds for a variety of research, service, and developmental activities. During this time, he has served as both editor and editorial board member of several professional journals, and he has authored a variety of grant proposals, professional articles, and annual performance reports. His grants have ranged from $5,000 to over $1 million with more than $35 million in grant support to date.

In addition to administering funded projects, Brewer has taught graduate courses in the areas of grantwriting, project design, project management and program evaluation, human resource management, continuous improvement and TQM, and self-directed work teams. He has given seminars, conducted workshops, and participated in a variety of grantwriting, project design, and program implementation workshops. A favorite workshop that he has repeatedly taught is his

"Principles of Learning" course. He also teaches noncredit courses that are available to community agency personnel and nonprofit organizations.

In teaching and supervising, his personal philosophy is to try to employ charisma, insight, and humor to create a contagious excitement for living, learning, and personal achievement. He does this by employing the various *13 Proven Ways to Get Your Message Across* presented in this book.

Introduction

The 13 techniques included in this book have proved successful in the classroom, at conference meetings, in workshops, and on retreats. They have been equally useful with one or two participants and with audiences of several hundred. Whether you are a teacher, a trainer, a guest speaker, a seminar leader, or a team leader designated to bring an idea to the executive committee, this book is for you. Any of these 13 presentation techniques may be appropriate for a given learning session—depending on the topic, the size of the audience, and the personality and style of the presenter. You may wish to observe and learn some of these techniques by watching other effective trainers and teachers in action.

You may ask, "How can I use these techniques in my presentations?" Some readers may want to consider the techniques, select one to experiment with, and, after the session, evaluate themselves on their effectiveness. I do not pretend to exhaust the range of possibilities with these techniques. Rather, I focus on several examples that I have come to value for their versatility and effectiveness in my 18-plus years of teaching in a major research university and making presentations and conducting workshops in the business community and at a 2-year community college.

The contents of each chapter will be of considerable value to individuals who are preparing for teaching or training careers at any level of instruction—middle school, high school, or college—or for training individuals in the work environment. Many experienced teachers and trainers may also find that the various techniques provide criteria for technical decisions they must make regarding classroom instruction. Also, this collection is for those who work as consultants or advisers to teachers. An effort has been made to provide a general and, to some extent, conceptual analysis of practices in teaching and presenting. My intention and hope is that the book will provide trainers, teachers, and others concerned with instruction some general guidelines for thinking about instructional practice. Throughout the book, the choice of techniques does not dictate what the classroom practitioner ought to do. Peculiarities in teaching situations vary so widely that it seems ill advised to attempt to prescribe practices that should be universally and literally implemented.

One aspect of a presenter's work is to exercise skill in judgment and apply his or her specialized knowledge to fashion the specifics of the teaching practice.

A Word About the
Planning and Evaluation Sheets

To assist the classroom practitioner in using the 13 techniques included in this book, I have developed planning and evaluation sheets for each respective technique that are placed at the end of each chapter. Planning is an essential aspect of any quality presentation. The planning worksheet will assist classroom practitioners in thinking through and preparing for the technique they plan to use. It will be a helpful reference to the concepts and objectives of the session and a reminder of materials and equipment needs. Finally, this page may serve as the session outline.

The evaluation sheet will help educators who are concerned about their own professional development assess their effectiveness after each training session. Another valuable source of feedback is from the individual learners. Each prospective trainer and trainee can offer valuable insights for improving the teaching and learning process. It is recommended, therefore, that the lecturer use this sheet for self-evaluation and that he or she also request similar feedback from the audience to validate self-perceptions and reveal any discrepancies.

A Word About
How to Use the Checklist

The selection of a teaching technique involves consideration of the learners (number, background, experience), the desired cognitive outcomes, and appropriate sensory involvement. Use of the checklist on page 12 will facilitate the classroom practitioner's task of choosing the best technique for a given situation. Each instructional method presented in this volume (listed in the left-hand column of the checklist) has been marked according to the appropriate cognitive levels (as identified in Bloom's taxonomy) and according to the type(s) of sensory involvement which would be (or could be) helpful in using that technique.

An excellent step-by-step method for using this book would be to (1) consider the learning needs and desired outcomes for a training session, (2) use this checklist to select one or two appropriate techniques, (3) turn to the chapter(s) treating the preferred strategies, (4) read the chapters, and (5) make a final selection.

What Are Teaching and Learning?

The teacher performs many tasks during the course of a school day or a training session. Although some of those activities take place in the absence of participants or students, teaching occurs when the classroom practitioner interacts with one or more participants, with the intent that the participants learn from the encounter. The teacher or trainer directs participants to do certain things with the expectation that they will learn from the activity. Some educational scholars compare teaching and learning with buying and selling. The analogy of teaching and selling is a coordinate concept, but the analogy of learning and buying is not. Nevertheless, one can conclude that selling is possible only if there are buyers. Similarly, one cannot teach unless another is receiving instruction and, hopefully, learning.

The Basic Laws of Learning

The laws of learning fall into two main categories: primary and secondary. The primary laws consist of the laws of readiness, of exercise or repetition (including drill and practice), and of effect. The three secondary laws are the laws of primacy, intensity, and regency. Malone (1991) noted that educational pioneers such as Edward Lee Thorndike and John Broadus Watson refer to other laws as well. For example, there are the laws of set or attitude, associative shifting, and analogy.

With regard to the primary laws, the *law of readiness* informs the classroom practitioner that when a participant is ready to learn and that person can connect experiences he or she has had in the past with the knowledge to be acquired, optimal learning may result. Readiness implies that a person is eager to learn what is being presented or addressed in the workshop. Participants typically learn with greater facility when they are able to associate some of their past experiences with new material. They also must be interested and motivated in order to learn. This eagerness must precede the introduction of content. The classroom practitioner often can establish this state of readiness by helping participants see the need to learn or the value of what is to be presented.

The second primary law, the *law of exercise,* informs educators of the importance of practice and repetition. Ordinarily, participants must practice what they are learning if they are to remember it. It is most important that participants be given the opportunity to practice or repeat the skills and knowledge they are expected to retain.

The final primary law is the *law of effect,* which Mazur (1990) references in his book. This law suggests that learning and retention are strengthened when the participant receives pleasure from the learning activity. Learning is weakened if participants experience displeasure with the activity. It is essential that individuals experience the content in a meaningful way and that they receive pleasure and satisfaction from the learning activities being presented. Presenters and teachers must therefore not only present material in such a manner as to engage the interest of participants, they must also avoid procedures that would be counterproductive. For example, if someone consistently interacts with the material in such a way that they experience failure, that individual will become far less interested in that particular learning experience. This also relates to the law of readiness, because in order to interact productively with the material, the learner must be in a state of readiness.

The secondary laws of primacy and recency are somewhat self-explanatory. For example, the *law of primacy* reminds us of the importance of first impressions. Typically, what is learned at the beginning of a session is remembered best. Often, learning that occurs at the end is also retained well. The middle segment of a presentation will have less impact unless the presenter or teacher finds a way to highlight that segment in the learner's memory. The law of recency suggests that the stronger the connection, the more intense the learning will be between the stimuli and the response. One aid for this may be found in another of the secondary laws, the *law of intensity.*

In working with the law of intensity, the classroom practitioner attempts to make the experience vivid and exciting. Scintillating activities are certainly more likely to be retained than mundane ones. At times, this presents a special challenge, because the educator also must remember the primary law dealing with the need for exercise, or repetition.

The *law of regency* should be considered throughout the learning process. When considering the material or skill that is most important, one must select carefully the activities and their timing. Otherwise, the result may be that basic information or other learning does not make optimum impact on participants. The main part of a learning experience ideally will be highlighted in the memories of learners through the strategic selection and timing of activities.

As mentioned earlier, the educational scholars Thorndike and Watson alluded to other laws, such as the *law of set or attitude.* An example of working with this law is that competent instructors begin the instruction with an anticipatory set—that is, a brief activity designed to gain participant's attention and get them focused on the topic. This focus must be a matter of both mind and attitude. Thorndike's (1905) *law of effect* refers to a personal and cultural predisposition to behave in a particular way in a particular situation. There is also the *law of analogy,* which considers transfer of successful responses from one environment to another.

Another law alluded to by Thorndike is the *law of multiple responses*. This law states that if one response does not solve a problem, another response will be tried. Although some of these concepts are better understood and may have greater applicability in a given setting than others, the educator will be well advised to adhere to these general principles or laws when preparing for each learning session.

Teaching in the Cognitive, Affective, and Psychomotor Domains

Two major handbooks provide extensive information on these taxonomies. B. S. Bloom's (1956) *Taxonomy of Educational Objectives—Handbook I* focuses on the cognitive domain. Krathwohl, Bloom, and Masia's (1964) *Taxonomy of Educational Objectives—Handbook II* followed later and provides detailed information on the affective domain. Simpson (1972) classified the major classifications of the psychomotor domain that currently are used extensively by classroom practitioners.

Most educators and trainers are familiar with Bloom's taxonomy of critical thinking skills. Hunter (1990) noted that Bloom separated cognition into six levels. His cognitive domain classification includes receiving information (knowledge), comprehension, application, analysis, synthesis, and evaluation. Many of these thinking skills are self-explanatory. One who is present at a lecture or a panel discussion, for example, first receives and then hopefully comprehends the information. In such educational settings (lectures or panels) there may be little opportunity to think at a higher level because the flow of information does not allow for it. Strategies such as role-playing, inquiry, and case study are slower in pace and require much more sophisticated thought processes. For example, in a case study the participants must apply their knowledge to the given study as they seek a solution to the problem. In doing so, they analyze the facts and synthesize the given information with (or integrate it into) their prior knowledge. Participants likely will propose numerous alternatives, evaluate the possibilities, and select the one that their analysis indicates is the best answer to the problem. As noted on the chart on page 12, those strategies that require complex thinking are generally conducted in small-group settings. Strategies such as the case study, the inquiry method, and questioning are most effective when the size of the group permits active involvement of everyone.

Henson (1996) defines *affective domain* as the part of "human learning that involves changes in interests, attitudes, and values" p. 57. Krathwohl, Bloom, and Masia (1964) classified the affective domain into five major categories—receiving, responding, valuing, organizing, and characterizing. The affective domain represents a powerful means of learning because it deals with attitudes, values, feelings, and interests. Affective learning is a continuous process that goes beyond the typical classroom environment. Role-playing, group discussion, and brainstorming are some of the teaching techniques noted in this book that represent excellent ways to get participants to deal with safety issues, attitudes toward change, and so on. After individuals are made aware of an issue (receiving), the next higher level is to get them to attend or react to it (responding). They then need to value it. For example, an employee will recognize the worth of other coworkers by giving assistance without being asked, working cooperatively with them, using tact in replying to coworkers, and sharing ideas freely with them. Hohn (1995) noted that attitudes and values that are initially external to an individual have yet to be learned to the point of becoming part of a person's habit pattern. He noted that in "information-processing terms, learning in the early stages of the taxonomy is not yet based on an interconnected network of schemas. As additional experience is integrated into cognitive structure, however, affective learning at the later stages of the taxonomy is considered to be internal, or part of the individual's habitual way of perceiving and responding to the environment" (Hohn, 1995, pp. 301-302). It should be noted that affective learning does not occur independently nor is it taught in isolation from the cognitive domain.

The *psychomotor domain* consists of five major categories—imitation, manipulation, precision, articulation, and naturalization (Armstrong, 1970). *Kinesthetic* or psychomotor domain learning involves movement that is required or that in some way facilitates the learning process. Development of sports skills is an obvious area in which physical movement plays a major role in learning. Movement and manipulation of equipment and materials are several of the 13 strategies discussed in this book. Demonstration, when the session calls for participants to replicate the presentation, is an activity that utilizes the kinesthetic domain. Practically speaking, any activity that involves tactile learning probably also calls for kinesthetic activity. Lazear (1991) makes use of kinesthetic learning to teach vocabulary. This is accomplished by introducing the words (unfamiliar to the participants) and providing physical movements (without words) as the definition. Participants observe and then practice the motions associated with the vocabulary words. Afterwards, participants are shown a group of definitions and find, perhaps to their surprise, that they are able to associate the verbal definitions with the appropriate vocabulary words. Creative classroom practitioners find opportunities to include this domain for variety and effectiveness in the teaching and learning process.

Environment and Effective Learning

Teaching ordinarily occurs when the teacher interacts with one or more learners. However, feelings, emotions, or attitudes may block learning. Classroom practitioners cannot begin to dispel all of these blocks, but they must address some of them, especially boredom, confusion, irritability, and fear among the participants.

How the classroom is set up can either facilitate or impede the learning process. Use of space, the seating arrangements, and other environmental factors influence the attitudes of both presenter and learners. The physical setting sets the tone. As much as possible, the trainer or instructor must monitor the appropriateness of lighting, temperature, noise level, and space in an attempt to ensure that these environmental factors are helpful rather than detrimental. Assessment of the physical environment must be ongoing throughout the session.

In addition, it is important to recognize the importance of the trainer's mental attitude as an environmental factor. Individuals who approach their responsibilities with enthusiasm for the subject, confidence in their abilities, and appropriate preparation for the session will be well on their way to avoiding blocks to learning. If the teacher also demonstrates genuine acceptance of each of the participants, this quality—together with adequate preparation—should help avoid or eliminate the learning deterrents that can be managed and controlled by the classroom practitioner.

Effective Teaching Skills

That which is seen as effective teaching or presenting by one observer may be considered poor by another. This phenomenon occurs because each person's values and experiences are different from everyone else's. However, although it may be difficult to come to agreement about what good presenting or teaching is, effective teaching can be demonstrated. The effective classroom practitioner is an individual who is able to bring about intended outcomes in a consistent manner.

Although the nature of learning is itself important, different classroom practitioners may seek and achieve favorable outcomes using different techniques. All of these classroom practitioners would be judged effective. This leads us to the prime criterion for assessment of effective teaching or training—a positive correlation between intent and outcome. Thus, if we exclude intent, participants' achievements would be random or accidental, and if participants at presentations do not achieve the intended outcomes, the trainer or teacher cannot be considered effective.

Smith (1969) noted that a teacher who is well trained is prepared in four major areas. First, this teacher has command of the theoretical knowledge of human behavior and learning. This includes motivation and reinforcement techniques. Second, the teacher displays a positive attitude toward the subject matter and the participants, in order to foster learning and development. Third, the teacher possesses command of the subject area that she or he will be presenting. This subject knowledge includes not only presentation methods but the implementation, evaluation, and feedback phases as well. Finally, the well-trained teacher employs technical strategies that result in meaningful learning experiences, such as those outlined in this book.

Classroom practitioners must be able to make solid decisions concerning (a) content selection, (b) appropriate involvement by participants, (c) demonstration that appropriate learning has occurred, and (d) the presenter's role as facilitator of learning. Effective trainers and teachers must plan, implement, and evaluate themselves as well as their participants in order to hone their skills.

Planning is perhaps the most important strategy for assuring better presentations and teaching. As the old saying goes, "It wasn't raining when Noah built the ark." Noah planned ahead; so must teachers and other presenters. Essential aspects of planning include determining the learning objectives, content, and teaching techniques and deciding what participants must do in order to demonstrate that learning has occurred. One also must consider the anticipatory set, wherein the trainer gains the attention and interest of learners, and the closure, during which the classroom practitioner brings the session to an appropriate conclusion.

Qualities of Effective
Trainers and Educators

Successful presenters and educators have in common several key characteristics. These may be categorized under traits of character and personality, interpersonal skills, expectations of self and students, possession of an adequate knowledge base, instructional skills and methods, and classroom management skills. Numerous surveys have found that the most effective educators are perceived as caring, enthusiastic, consistent, and impartial in their dealings with students.

The adage "They won't care what you know 'til they know that you care" fits here. If participants believe the classroom practitioner cares about them and about their learning, they also will attribute other important character and personality traits to the classroom practitioner—such as being patient and sensitive to their needs and having a sense of purpose. When demonstrated, these qualities in the trainer help students have a positive disposition toward learning and meet the classroom practitioner's expectations.

Excellent classroom practitioners expect their participants to have high standards of behavior and academic achievement. These classroom practitioners expect participants to provide appropriate feedback and to be involved in their own learning, as opposed to being passive in class. Trainers and teachers expect students to be prepared for learning sessions and to follow through with review and practice on their own, to further enhance their growth.

Master trainers and educators likewise have high expectations of themselves. They see themselves as self-reliant directors and facilitators of learning and as role models. They have well-defined personal goals. They are rigorous in self-appraisal and work consistently toward even greater personal development.

Proficient educators possess excellent communication skills, get along well with others, are capable leaders, and are able to persuade participants to extend themselves beyond former boundaries. They readily establish rapport with students and other professionals. They learn participants' names as quickly as possible and make a practice of addressing students by name. Their caring attitude is felt in their appreciation of the unique characteristics of each student and in their encouragement of participants to expect the best of themselves. In addition, master trainers and educators are able to bring a sense of humor to the task. They are ethical, respectful of others, and appropriately assertive as they engage students in the learning process.

Obviously, excellent classroom presenters must possess a mastery of their particular discipline. They usually exhibit special talents in their area of expertise. They continue to update themselves in their content areas and develop new skills and strategies of instruction. Expert teachers recognize the importance of appropriate pacing so that difficult concepts are dealt with more slowly and review is fast paced. Master teachers give directions clearly and in logical sequence. Competent educators make frequent checks for understanding and provide for individual learning differences despite environmental variables. They encourage students and participants in their workshops to go beyond the elementary learning of information and be able to apply their knowledge and practice the higher-order thinking skills of analysis, synthesis, and evaluation. They encourage participants' questions. They also refer students to other sources, rather than have them rely solely on a single textbook.

Finally, proficient educators, whether in the classroom or in other settings, find appropriate ways to support participants in their efforts to gain insights, and they always attempt to reward improvement and success. They incorporate diverse teaching strategies and use effective audiovisuals to enhance learning. They respect partici- pants' points-of-view, create readiness to learn by helping participants see how the material will be useful to them, and assist students in transferring new learning. They illustrate abstract concepts with real- life examples.

To accomplish all this, trainers and teachers must possess much energy and enthusiasm. They need to be expressive, making use of eye contact, moving appropriately toward their students, and ges- turing appropriately as they communicate. Energy is evident long before students and instructor meet, for effective educators invest themselves in planning and developing a variety of instructional strat- egies, such as the 13 presented in this book. They avoid merely trying to "wing it."

Effective presenters are careful to avoid meaningless motions of their hands, which might confuse listeners. They keep their hands out of their pockets, avoid leaning on the podium except as a point of emphasis or intensity, and avoid disruptive pacing back and forth. They do gesture and move about the room, but with purpose rather than as evidence of nervousness.

Conclusion

This book is presented with several purposes in mind: to (1) help individuals become better educators, (2) serve as an ongoing reference for teaching fundamentals, and (3) challenge experienced teachers to expand their repertoire of skills in working with their vari- ous audiences. Veterans of the profession may find new teaching methods in this book. Teachers and trainers who are just beginning will find a ready source that contains a wide variety of teaching tech- niques. Instructions are detailed enough for novices to select and implement them, using the planning sheets at the end of each chap- ter. Evaluation sheets on the pages following the planning sheets should be used for further growth and development.

This volume contains methods for working with a wide range of learners—from individual instruction offered to persons encoun- tering the material for the first time to audiences for whom the learn- ing session is an enrichment experience. It includes techniques that lead students and trainees to develop new skills and methods for presenting to larger groups an abundance of information in a logical, interesting fashion. I trust and hope that this book will be useful to all educators seeking to improve their teaching techniques.

References

Armstrong, R. J. (1970). *Developing and writing behavioral objectives.* Tucson, AZ: Educational Innovators Press.

Bloom, B. S. (1976). *Human characteristics and school learning.* New York: McGraw-Hill.

Bloom, B. S., Englehart, M. B., Furst, E. J., Hill, W. H., & Krathwohl, D. R. (1956). *Taxonomy of educational objectives: The classification of educational goals. Handbook I: Cognitive domain.* New York: Longman Green.

Henson, K. T. (1996). *Methods and strategies for teaching in secondary and middle schools* (3rd ed.). New York: Longman.

Hohn, R. L. (1995). *Classroom learning and teaching.* New York: Longman.

Hunter, M. (1990). *Mastery teaching.* El Segundo, CA: TIP.

Krathwohl, D. R., Bloom, B. S., & Masia, B. B. (1964). *Taxonomy of educational objectives. Handbook II: Affective domain.* New York: David McKay.

Lazear, D. (1991). *Seven ways of knowing: Teaching for multiple intelligences.* Palatine, IL: Skylight.

Mazur, J. E. (1990). *Learning and behavior* (2nd ed.). Englewood Cliffs, NJ: Prentice Hall.

Malone, J. C. (1991). *Theories of learning: A historical approach.* Belmont, CA: Wadsworth.

Simpson, E. J. (1972). *The classification of educational objectives in the psychomotor domain. The psychomotor domain* (Vol. 3). Washington, DC: Gryphon House.

Smith, B. O. (1969). *Teachers for the real world.* Washington, DC: American Association of Colleges for Teacher Education.

Thorndike, E. L. (1905). *The elements of psychology.* New York: Seiler.

Checklist According to Cognitive Outcomes and Sensory Involvement

Instructional Technique

	Lecture	Small-Group Discussion	Role-Playing	Case Study	Demonstration	Panel	Inquiry Method	Buzz Groups	Programmed Instruction	Directed Study	Experiment	Brainstorming	Questioning
Cognitive Levels													
Information	●	●	●	●	●	●	●		●	●	●	●	●
Comprehension	●	●	●	●	●	●	●		●	●	●	●	●
Application			●	●	●	●	●	●	●	●	●	●	●
Analysis		●	●	●	●	●	●	●	●	●	●	●	●
Synthesis		●	●	●	●	●	●	●	●	●	●	●	●
Evaluation		●	●	●	●	●	●	●	●	●	●	●	●
Sensory Appeal													
Auditory (sound)	●	●	●	●	●	●	●	●	●	●	●	●	●
Visual (sight)	●	●	●	●	●		●		●		●	●	●
Tactile (touch)			●		●		●				●		
Olfactory (smell)					●						●		
Gustatory (taste)					●						●		
Instructional Methods When You Want to. . .													
Only Give Information	●					●							
Encourage Participation		●	●		●	●	●	●	●	●	●	●	●
Provide Hands-on Experience					●					●	●		
Get Participants to Respond		●	●	●	●	●	●	●				●	●
Have Participants Simulate Interpersonal Communications		●	●	●	●		●	●				●	●
Give Problem-Solving Opportunities to Participants		●	●	●	●		●	●				●	●
Instructional Method According to Teaching and Learning													
Teaching Method	●				●	●			●				
Teaching Method to Aid Learning								●				●	●
Learning Method			●	●			●				●	●	
Teaching-Learning Method		●			●								

1
Lecture

Definition

The lecture is a method of presenting facts, information, or principles verbally with little or no participation from the audience. The lecture is a carefully prepared talk given by a qualified person.

Introduction

The lecture is a traditional teaching method that has been criticized because it provides no opportunity for the audience to participate in the presentation. Telling people what you want them to know, however, is still one of the most common methods of teaching.

When using the lecture, the expert in the field gives an organized, in-depth presentation to the audience. The presentation of a lecture can be formal or informal and can be accompanied by the use of audiovisual aids. It is a convenient method for presenting a large amount of information to an audience in a relatively short time.

Main Procedural Steps
in Using the Lecture

The procedure for using the lecture technique begins with careful preparation on the part of the presenter. For the lecture technique to be effective, the presenter must know his or her subject matter. Any attempt to learn as you go will be easily identified in the lecture presentation.

Once the presenter is prepared, the lecture is simply a matter of presenting the material to the audience in a way that will keep them interested and get the material across clearly. To do this, the following steps must be taken.

Step 1: Outline Your Presentation

Careful preparation is essential because the presenter will lose his or her audience at the first sign of rambling. Every good lecture begins with a good outline. The outline will not only keep the presenter focused but also provide a good checkpoint for the listeners. Share your outline with the audience by telling them what points you are going to cover and then talking about each point in order. Keep the outline simple so it doesn't become a distraction from your lecture.

Step 2: Keep It Simple

Most audiences can only absorb a few main ideas at each sitting. Generally, two to four main ideas should be the maximum presented during a lecture. Although the concepts can be complicated, the structure of the lecture should be kept simple.

A good start can set the tone for the whole lecture. It also helps to establish the purpose of the lecture both in your mind and in the mind of the listeners. The introduction should be carefully planned and as interesting as possible.

Audiences listen better and retain more when they know what to listen for and what the purpose is. Spell out your objectives at the beginning. Repeat them at the end.

Repetition is important for retention. Important points need to be repeated at least three times in order to be remembered.

Step 3: Use a Conversational Approach

Conversational style is important to the lecture process. The presenter should know his or her audience and tailor the lecture to their level. This includes avoiding unfamiliar words and stiff formal presentations. Brewer and Traver (1976) support using humor, anecdotes and visual aids to help keep the audience alert and involved in the lecture process.

The presenter should arrange his or her material so that the ideas are expressed clearly. Be specific. Use short sentences for emphasis. Terms such as *however, nevertheless, then* and *finally* are important transitions for the listeners.

Step 4: Vary Your Speech Rate

Audience interest and retention depends upon how well the material is presented. An average of 100 to 150 words per minute is considered a safe speed for oral presentation. The lecturer should remember to slow down for more difficult material, present simple material at a faster rate, and pause often so that the listeners can comprehend what is being said.

Step 5: Show Enthusiasm

An appropriate level of enthusiasm conveys the presenter's attitude toward the subject matter. If the presenter demonstrates a high level of enthusiasm, the audience will tap into this energy and be encouraged to listen. Presentation and delivery are keys in sustaining participants' interest. Bellon, Bellon, and Blank (1992) link presenter enthusiasm with participant achievement through the use of varied voice level, energy, body gestures, eye contact, facial expression, and descriptive words.

Step 6: Show Physical Behavior

Moving freely around the front of the room can be a great aid in keeping your audience alert. However, some mannerisms are distracting and run the risk of becoming the focus, rather than the lecture. Leaning on the podium or playing with coins, papers, or a pointer are examples of distracting mannerisms.

Keep good eye contact. Look at the audience in the same way you would if you were carrying on a conversation with them.

Step 7: Keep the Purpose of the Lecture Clearly in Mind

Before beginning the lecture or the outline, write down the purpose of the lecture. This purpose should be specific.

It is helpful to begin with an advanced organizer—a new introductory idea or concept that can be incorporated by the audience with their existing knowledge of a subject. This helps the lecturer show the audience how his or her information is important to them, thus clarifying the purpose. Joyce, Weil, and Showers (1992) agree that if an appropriate advance organizer is chosen, accompanied by a strong delivery of organized information, successful learning will occur.

If the lecturer doesn't know his or her purpose, the listeners will have a difficult time understanding the lecture.

Step 8: Use Audiovisual Materials and Follow-up Groups

The pure lecture can be greatly enhanced by the use of charts, graphs, handouts, filmstrips, pictures, models, chalkboards, and other interest-arousing aids. Brookfield (1990) suggests that another way to spark interest is to end the lecture with a question related to the topic to initiate a thought-provoking free flow of ideas among individuals within a group. Follow up the lecture with buzz groups or discussion groups. Interactive discussion allows the listeners to clarify and retain the material.

Variations of the Lecture

The pure lecture has a few variations. Lectures can be formal or informal and can be given in person, by tape recording, or on videotape.

A *formal lecture* is most effective (useful) when introducing new or complicated concepts or ideas or when there is a need to cover several concepts or ideas in a short period of time. The formal lecture is usually given to large groups. The presenter will lecture during the entire allotted time with little or no interaction from the audience.

The formal lecture can be greatly enhanced by techniques that offer some audience participation. Such techniques include the use of the informal lecture, audiovisual aids, and discussion groups.

An *informal lecture* is designed for smaller groups and lends itself to more interaction with the audience. The presenter can encourage questions and comments and still maintain the lecture format.

Another variation of the informal lecture is the lecture forum. The lecture forum is a talk given by a qualified person that is followed by open discussion with other experts.

Appropriate Uses, Suggestions, and Cautions

Because the lecture is a passive form of learning, it must be used carefully and not overused. The lecture technique is best used under the following circumstances:

✓ When the audience is large
✓ When there are many ideas to present in a short period of time
✓ When the information is not readily available because the topic is too current for textbooks
✓ When introducing a new subject

✓ When summarizing or giving directions
✓ When presenting analysis of a controversial issue (however, here the lecture is more likely to be called a speech)

Points to watch when using the lecture method include the following:

✓ Know the material.
✓ Know your audience and watch for signs of fatigue or disinterest.
✓ Keep the number of points to to a minimum.
✓ Keep the presentation simple and conversational, avoiding unfamiliar words and long sentences.
✓ Present summaries at the beginning and end.

The informal lecture is especially good for smaller groups and encourages the audience to ask questions and add their comments. Because it is not a discussion group, the lecturer can still maintain control of the information being presented but keep the listeners interested by asking questions. The questions can be designed for the listeners to answer on the spot, or they can be rhetorical questions— ones the lecturer asks, then answers.

The use of audiovisual aids has become extremely popular in the lecture method. Whether it is an overhead projector with computer-enhanced graphics or the chalkboard, the audiovisual adds a helpful learning style or aid to the lecture method. Brewer, Hollingsworth, and Campbell (1995) and Parker (1993) suggest that lectures should use visual imagery that ties in with the words in the lecture so the viewer can retrieve a mental picture of the subject to reinforce learning.

Discussion groups, sometimes called buzz sessions, are additions to the lecture method that help the presenter check to see if his or her message has been communicated effectively. Breaking into smaller groups to either complete an assignment—written or oral— or to discuss a particular issue that was covered in the lecture increases the effectiveness of this traditional teaching method. During the discussion, the lecturer should move from group to group, checking for comprehension.

Advantages, Disadvantages, and Limitations of the Lecture

When using the lecture instructional strategy, the presenter should be aware of the following advantages, disadvantages, and limitations of this technique.

Advantages of Lectures

1. Require little prior participant knowledge about subject matter
2. Material can be presented rapidly and logically
3. Convenient for large groups
4. Directions can be given clearly, therefore ensuring that all participants have the necessary information
5. Economical with classroom time because it immediately focuses the presenter's ideas
6. Easier for presenter to coordinate and control

Disadvantages of Lectures

1. The audience is less likely to retain a large percentage of the material.
2. Overuse of lectures that are too long can lead to boredom on part of audience.
3. The possibility of miscommunication is greater.
4. Reflective thinking on the part of the audience is not encouraged.
5. Henson (1993) states that lectures are the least effective teaching method to promote long-term retention.

Limitations of Lectures

1. Not appropriate for hands-on type of skill training
2. Limited feedback from the audience
3. Puts responsibility for material on the presenter
4. Difficult to evaluate
5. Not appropriate for abstract, complex, or highly detailed material

Examples or Applications

Examples of the lecture include formal or informal classroom settings, after-dinner speeches, sermons, political speeches, and some training sessions.

The most effective application of the lecture is as a part of the whole. The lecture can be used for an introduction and as a summary. It can be especially effective when applied with other tools, such as audiovisual aids and limited discussion groups.

Summary

A lecture should be kept short and interesting, the presenter should have a concrete knowledge of the subject matter, and the presentation should be well organized. When used properly, the lecture can be an effective teaching tool. It is most successful when used informally and enhanced by other methods, such as audiovisual aids and discussion groups. Gilstrap and Martin (1975) note the range for the lecture method by noting that the lecture can "challenge the imagination of each student, arouse curiosity, develop his [or her] spirit of inquiry, and encourage his [or her] creativity" (p. 7).

References

Bellon, J., Bellon, E., & Blank, M. (1992). *Teaching from a research knowledge base*. New York: Merrill.

Brewer, E. W., Hollingsworth, C., & Campbell, A. (1995). Accelerated learning and short-term instructional programs: Sustaining interest and intrapersonal growth. *Southeastern Association of Educational Opportunity Program Personnel Journal, 14*(1), 57-85.

Brewer, E. W., & Traver, G. J. (1978). *The funniest jokes*. Bend, OR: Maverick.

Brookfield, S. D. (1990). *The skillful teacher*. San Francisco: Jossey-Bass.

Gilstrap, R. L., & Martin, W. R. (1975). *Current strategies for teachers*. Pacific Palisades, CA: Goodyear.

Henson, K. T. (1993). *Methods and strategies for teaching in secondary and middle schools*. New York: Longman.

Joyce, B., Weil, M., & Showers, B. (1992). *Models of teaching*. Boston: Allyn & Bacon.

Parker, J. K. (1993). Lecturing and loving it. *The Clearing House, 67*(1), 8-10.

The Lecture Planning Sheet

Date:_____ Time:_____ Site:_____

Intended Audience:

Topic Statement:

Objective(s) of Session:

Main Ideas of Lecture:

      1.

      2.

      3.

      4.

      5.

Media Needed:

Handouts:

Follow-up Activity(ies):

Summary Notes:

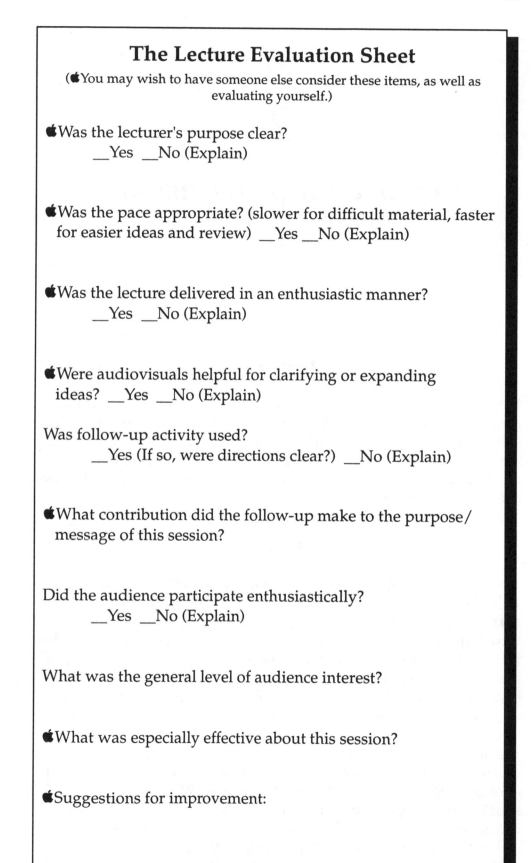

The Lecture Evaluation Sheet

(You may wish to have someone else consider these items, as well as evaluating yourself.)

Was the lecturer's purpose clear?
__Yes __No (Explain)

Was the pace appropriate? (slower for difficult material, faster for easier ideas and review) __Yes __No (Explain)

Was the lecture delivered in an enthusiastic manner?
__Yes __No (Explain)

Were audiovisuals helpful for clarifying or expanding ideas? __Yes __No (Explain)

Was follow-up activity used?
__Yes (If so, were directions clear?) __No (Explain)

What contribution did the follow-up make to the purpose/ message of this session?

Did the audience participate enthusiastically?
__Yes __No (Explain)

What was the general level of audience interest?

What was especially effective about this session?

Suggestions for improvement:

2

Small-Group Discussion

Definition

Small-group discussion allows presenters to announce a topic or idea for group discussion among participants. A small-group discussion follows democratic guidelines and allows everyone to contribute many ideas for others to discuss and reflect upon. Discussion allows for an interchange of ideas within the context of a group under the direction of a presenter.

Introduction

Whenever groups of people congregate in the same place, they will talk with one another. It is human nature to be curious about our surroundings and other people, and the best way to find out answers to our questions is to talk with one another. A discussion may be information based, concentrating on facts, or it may focus on personal opinion and feelings. People enjoy discussions and the arenas of thought they uncover. Talking with friends reveals attitudes and values and offers insight into ways of solving personal problems.

New ideas can be evaluated and tested using the discussion method. Small-group discussions, under the guidance of a presenter, discuss issues to achieve understanding and consensus after much consideration of the viewpoints and ideas of others. Its goals are to spark new thought and concept exploration, encourage analysis of factual information, and develop open-mindedness toward new attitudes and beliefs, so as to accept the opinions of others.

Small-group discussions serve intellectual, emotional, and social purposes. Intellectually, discussion helps participants become aware of the diversity of opinions on an issue. It also allows participants to realize the complexity of issues when they walk away from a discussion with more questions than when they went into the discussion. This is good because it helps them to think about all the possibilities. The participants must discern the difference between fact and opinion and thus they must practice the skill of listening.

Emotionally, the participants may have some sort of personal involvement in the issue they are discussing, making it important to them. Others should be sensitive to this. Participants want others to realize that their opinions matter, and once the group responds to this, each participant retains a feeling of self-worth. This is an important affective quality that is key to the building of self-confidence and a sense of belonging.

Socially, group discussion builds a sense of cohesion and trust with one another. Discussion groups are an arena in which differences in opinion, race, gender, and participation should be accepted and celebrated. Differences allow for the diffusion of new ideas and attitudes. Group work of any sort helps participants build their interpersonal skills and confidence about offering individual opinions in a group atmosphere.

A well-conducted group discussion will end in acceptance of different opinions, respect for well-supported beliefs, and improved problem-solving skills. Overall, it will promote the sharing of information and all members will gain insight concerning the thoughts of others before reaching consensus on a topic. Bellon, Bellon, and Blank (1992) believe participants in small groups concentrate better on the topic at hand due to the support of their peers and individual motivation.

Main Procedural Steps in Using Small-Group Discussion

The purpose of the small-group discussion is to contribute and circulate information on a particular topic and analyze and evaluate the information for supported evidence in order to reach an agreement on general conclusions. To do this, several steps must be taken when conducting small-group discussions.

Step 1: Introduction

The presenter must prepare before the discussion for it to be successful. The presenter should try to introduce a topic on which all of the participants have some background knowledge so they have a basis for discussion. If the participants are introduced to a topic that is familiar to them, each will have something to contribute that another participant may not have thought of, thus moving the discussion on its way with many new avenues of thought to explore. The introduction should have four parts.

1. *Instructional Objective.* An instructional objective should be given to the participants at the beginning of the discussion.
2. *Purpose.* The presenter should explain why the groups will be discussing the chosen topic.
3. *Relationship.* The presenter must explain how this information fits in with what has already been learned or what will be learned in the future.
4. *Advanced Organizer.* An advanced organizer is some sort of attention-grabber that attracts participants' interest. Many discussion topics fail because participants aren't drawn into the discussion at the beginning.

The presenter may have to help the participants understand how small-group discussion works to help them make the most of their time. Participants must understand the difference between a discussion and an unguided expression of opinion without pertinent information or facts. Participants might have to do a little research beforehand to get acquainted with the presenter's selected topic. Brookfield (1990) suggests choosing topics that are not too fact oriented or lacking in controversy to spark creative thought and diverse responses.

Step 2: Directing the Discussion

The presenter is in charge of directing the discussion to get it started. The presenter should ask the participants if they have questions about the topic at hand. These questions can start the discussion, or the presenter may want to ask a few questions from a prepared list to stimulate thought toward the topic. Another way to begin the discussion is to ask the participants to recall and share personal events that have happened in their lives that relate to the topic. This is a good way to get everyone involved. Questions are excellent motivators for discussion.

Sometimes the participants will take different thought paths and deviate from the instructional objective, so the presenter might have to reroute the thinking. Leading questions from the presenter can direct the participants back to the topic. These questions should not be answered with a yes-or-no answer. They should contain key words and relate to the objective of the discussion. These presenter-guided questions will be a model for participants to ask of the peers in their group. King and Rosenshine (1993) found that participants who ask thought-provoking questions in small-group discussions encourage creative answers that increase the learning potential for all.

Once the discussion begins, questions are essential in keeping the discussion moving. They can bring the discussion back on track or emphasize an important concept. They can draw in shy or non-participating individuals and can be key in checking for understanding.

As the presenter directs the discussion, he or she should decide whether or not the participants are spending too much time on insignificant points. The presenter should try to keep control of the discussion, yet not dominate it. To avoid having the discussion centered around the presenter, he or she should try to enter in only when necessary.

Step 3: Summarizing the Discussion

Sometimes the participants may be confused or retain a wrong idea as right. The presenter should summarize to make sure the participants understand what has been discussed. For small-group discussions seeking consensus, it is important to summarize to make sure all the participants are thinking along the same lines. A final summary is essential at the end of the discussion. Conclusions should be recorded on the chalkboard so all can see them. The presenter should ask the participants how they would use the information. At times, a discussion will result in the participants' having incorrect ideas. Basically, summarization is helpful for clearing up confusion, covering main points, ending a discussion, and conveying consensus.

Variations of
Small-Group Discussion

Cooperative Learning Groups

In cooperative learning, a small group of participants works together to achieve a common goal. Cooperative learning operates on the premise that participants achieve more when they work together. The goals of cooperative learning are positive interdependence, face-to-face interaction among participants, individual accountability within the group, and interpersonal and small-group skills. This teaching method fosters cognitive development in the areas of retention and achievement and affective development through socialization and self-esteem. Henson (1993) notes that small-group discussions allow the participants to get to know each other on a personal level and give them a sense of belonging to a team.

Problem-Solving Groups

These groups exist in order to cooperate, discover, inquire, and think critically. For example, several participants might work together to solve mathematical problems through exploration. The purpose of the problem-solving groups is to approach real-life problems with an appropriate strategy. The participants find many approaches to the problem and test them for the best possible solution. Cooper (1990) states that problem-solving groups help participants come to logical solutions and make responsible decisions.

Group Investigation

The presenter breaks participants up into small groups based on particular interests. Each group has a certain category, and they gather information and analyze it for meaning. The participants then prepare and deliver a presentation to the class about what they discovered. The process teaches participants to work together, listen to one another, and support each others' work and opinions. This is a group-skill-building teaching method that strengthens peer interaction.

Appropriate Uses, Suggestions, and Cautions

The group discussion requires great skill on the part of the presenter. The presenter must encourage participants to participate freely and still keep the discussion on the topic. During the discussion, the presenter must help the participants to understand how all the opinions and facts relate to the topic. For the presenter to conduct the discussion successfully, he or she must carefully plan it in advance.

The presenter must identify the objectives of the discussion. These objectives should be relevant to the needs of the participant, and the participants should have some prior knowledge of the topic. An introduction should be used to explain to the participants why they need to accomplish this objective. The presenter should conduct the small-group discussion with leading questions. Summaries should be used by the presenter to check for agreement and understanding. Charts, models, or actual objects might help the participants understand what is being discussed.

A few cautions are in order. Some participants may want to talk all at once. The group will have to generate some sort of courtesy system to allow everyone to express his or her opinion at different times so all may hear. Some participants may not want to talk at all. The presenter may have to ask a few leading questions and encourage one of the more aggressive participants in the group to speak. One or two participants might monopolize the conversation. The presenter should explain the importance of letting everyone contribute. Some participants may strongly disagree on points and fight with one another. In this case, the presenter must carefully draw the topic to a neutral point so both may see the strengths and weaknesses of their arguments.

Advantages, Disadvantages, and Limitations of Small-Group Discussion

When using the small-group discussion, the presenter should be aware of the following advantages, disadvantages, and limitations of this instructional strategy.

Advantages of Small-Group Discussion

1. All participants in the group can participate.
2. It is a good way to get participants interested in a topic.
3. Participants may more easily understand another participant's explanation than a presenter's explanation.
4. The presenter can identify participants who need assistance.
5. The presenter can identify individual opinions about the topic.
6. It helps the participant see relationships among ideas or concepts related to the topic at hand (U. S. Professional Teacher Training, 1983).

Disadvantages of Small-Group Discussion

1. It is time-consuming.
2. Some participants in the group may do all the talking.
3. It involves less presenter involvement than other methods.
4. The discussion can easily get off track.

Limitations of Small-Group Discussion

1. It is not a method that transmits information or facts.
2. It involves more talk and less action.
3. The discussion must be carefully planned, not impulsive, to be effective.

Examples or Applications

The small-group discussion may have as its aim to come to some sort of definite goal or decision based on consensus; for example, "What is the best way for participants to study Shakespeare?" But small-group discussion can also be used for stimulating new ideas and insights without really aiming for a particular decision; for example, "What are some ethical guidelines politicians should follow?"

Each topic should begin with leading questions to direct participants in the desired pattern of thought toward a topic; for example, "What is the whole impact of recycling on a global basis, and what actions can we take to continue this renewing process?" or "How serious is the damage we have done to our earth?" or "What can we do individually or collectively to make a difference?"

Summary

Small-group discussion develops the cognitive and affective abilities of participants. It is a process of freely sharing information and insights among peers in a welcoming environment under the guidance of a presenter. Individual effort is encouraged to make a strong team with creative ideas. Meloth and Deering (1994) note that groups are more likely to devote a collective effort toward their prescribed task and become more focused on their goal when in cooperative groups.

References

Bellon, J., Bellon, E., & Blank, M. (1992). *Teaching from a research knowledge base.* New York: Merrill.

Brookfield, S. (1990). *The skillful teacher.* San Francisco: Jossey-Bass.

Cooper, J. (1990). *Classroom teaching skills.* Toronto: D. C. Heath.

Henson, K. (1993). *Methods and strategies for teaching in secondary and middle schools.* New York: Longman.

King, A., & Rosenshine, B. (1993). Effects of guided cooperative questioning on children's knowledge construction. *Journal of Experimental Education, 6*(2), 127-147.

Meloth, M., & Deering, P. (1994). Task talk and task awareness under different cooperative learning conditions. *American Educational Research Journal, 31*(1), 138-165.

U. S. Professional Teacher Training. (1983). *Unit 2: Facilitate learning; PAK 5: Conduct a small group discussion.* (General Organization for Technical Education and Vocational Training). Riyadh, Kingdom of Saudi Arabia: Author.

The Small-Group Discussion Planning Sheet

Date:_____ Time:_____ Site:_____

Purpose Statement:

Specific Topic/Question to Be Discussed:

Relationship to Former/Future Learning:

Advanced Organizer:

Directions for Organizing Groups:

Directions for Discussion:

Plan for Sharing With Entire Assembly:

Handouts (if any):

Equipment (if any):

Summary Notes:

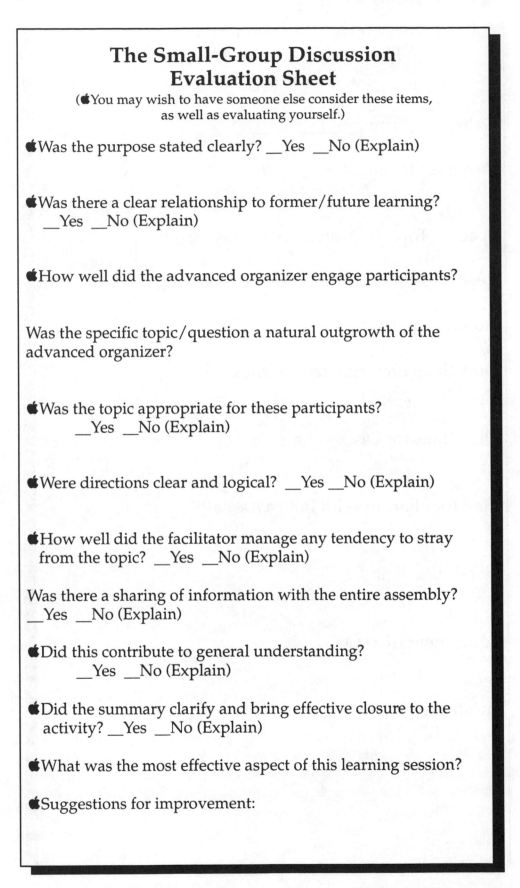

The Small-Group Discussion Evaluation Sheet

(You may wish to have someone else consider these items,
as well as evaluating yourself.)

Was the purpose stated clearly? __Yes __No (Explain)

Was there a clear relationship to former/future learning?
__Yes __No (Explain)

How well did the advanced organizer engage participants?

Was the specific topic/question a natural outgrowth of the
advanced organizer?

Was the topic appropriate for these participants?
__Yes __No (Explain)

Were directions clear and logical? __Yes __No (Explain)

How well did the facilitator manage any tendency to stray
from the topic? __Yes __No (Explain)

Was there a sharing of information with the entire assembly?
__Yes __No (Explain)

Did this contribute to general understanding?
__Yes __No (Explain)

Did the summary clarify and bring effective closure to the
activity? __Yes __No (Explain)

What was the most effective aspect of this learning session?

Suggestions for improvement:

3

Role-Playing

Definition

Role-playing is the spontaneous acting out of a problem, situation, or incident by members of a learning group. In role-playing, the actors assume the identity of another person or type of person and react to a situation in the manner that they believe their character would.

Introduction

Role-playing is a relatively new procedure in adult education and training but is one that children have been perfecting for decades. It is effective in getting people to better understand the emotions and behavior of others in a given situation.

Role-playing involves using realistic behavior in imaginary situations. In essence, it is "make believe," but the situations and problems must be real and relevant to real life. Because it requires spontaneous reactions on the part of the participants, no script is used. Considerable briefing and preparation on the part of the teacher, however, is essential for success.

Because role-playing captures the interest of the audience as well as the players, it also provides an excellent opportunity to develop skills in analysis and evaluation. Joyce, Weil, and Showers (1992) stated that role-playing examines individual feelings and actions, develops problem-solving techniques to combat social and personal problems, and helps one understand the feelings of others.

Main Procedural Steps
in Using Role-Playing

Before using the role-playing technique, the presenter should evaluate whether it is appropriate for the group of participants. Role-playing is most effective when

✓ The group is small
✓ The work under study deals with a problem or issue that involves feelings and attitudes rather than straight factual information
✓ The problem is capable of being solved by the participants
✓ There is more than one answer to the problem

There are two kinds of role-playing—structured and spontaneous. Structured role-playing involves prewritten cases selected from textbooks, personal experiences, or organizational training material. Structured role-playing usually emphasizes skill development.

Spontaneous role-playing involves no script. It is usually used to help participants gain insight into behavior and attitudes.

With structured and spontaneous role-playing, the presenter also has the option of deciding when the role-playing is to be introduced. Some presenters prefer to start with the general and move to the specific, therefore saving the role-playing until the theory discussions and lectures are over.

Other presenters lean more toward the "discovery" method. In that case, it is good to start with the role-playing exercise. Subsequent discussion would then refer back to the exercise, and group members can be encouraged to develop theories and ideas based on what they have seen.

The procedure for implementing role-playing involves six steps: planning, warm-up, implementation, enactment, discussion, and evaluation.

Step 1: Planning

Once the presenter has determined that role-playing is appropriate for the group, the next step is to select the topics. The problems should be carefully defined and should involve conditions that the members of the group will view as real and relevant. The role-playing situation should be typical of problems and conditions that the participants will face, not exaggerated or unrealistic conditions.

Step 2: Warm-up

Group motivation is very important. Especially with adults, the role-playing needs to be something that the group will relate to and not dismiss as preschool silliness.

The purpose of the warm-up is to get the group to participate in a constructive manner. The first obstacle to remove is any anxiety the members might have about role-playing. Following are several ways of reducing anxiety:

✓ Make the initial role-playing experience one of multiple roles involving three to five members.
✓ Explain carefully to the players what will happen during the role-playing session.
✓ Explain the role-playing process itself.
✓ Swink (1993) encourages the praise of risk taking to build confidence, and the occurrence of mistakes in order to learn from them.

In spontaneous role-playing, it is sometimes helpful to get the group involved in forming the problem to be discussed. A story or simple plot may be used to introduce the situation. Whenever possible, use volunteers to act out the roles. Because the audience will be directly involved in the analysis of the role-playing, it is not necessary to force group members who do not want to act to do so.

Two to five players are usually desirable for a single episode. Each character should have a name, and the roles should be discussed in private with each character. Other characters in the episode should not know what their counterparts will be doing or how they will be reacting.

When structured role-playing is used instead of spontaneous role-playing, warm-up can include a brief lecture, reading assignment, or filmstrip on the topic to be discussed.

Step 3: Implementation

Implementation consists of simply assigning roles and setting the boundaries for the role-playing. If there is a general instruction sheet of information that all the players and the audience need to know, it should be handed out or read aloud before the roles are assigned. Once assignments are made, the volunteers should be given a few minutes to read their scripts if it is a structured role-play. If it is a spontaneous role-play, a short time can be designated to review the characteristics the actors are to portray.

In spontaneous role-playing, characteristics should be kept confidential. Neither the other players nor the audience, for example, should know that "Mary's" character description says that she "always finds fault with new ideas."

While the role-players are studying, the presenter should either pass out "objective" sheets or inform the audience of the relevant things to look for in the role-playing. For example, the presenter may say, "Watch for any techniques that the supervisor uses in dealing with his or her employees."

The observer sheets may ask the audience to watch for such details as eye contact, body language, or overt hostility.

After the players have had a few minutes to review, the leader should then introduce each exercise with a brief statement, such as "Susan has asked her supervisor, Ernest, for a meeting to discuss a new computer program that she wants to purchase for her division."

Then let the enactment begin.

Step 4: Enactment

The true essence of role-playing comes to light in the enactment. Even in structured role-playing, it is the way the players carry out the assignment that enhances the learning technique. Their attitude, interpretation, and presentation are the springboards of the discussion to follow.

Keep the enactment moving with as few rules as possible. Exceptions are as follows:

✓ Keep the exercises short, no longer than 10 minutes for spontaneous role-playing and 15 minutes for structured. (Some prewritten, structured role-playing exercises run longer, but those should be considered special cases.)

✓ Stop the role-playing while interest is still high and before too much repetition starts to set in.

✓ Whenever possible, keep the role-playing going until key participants have had either a chance to respond two or three times or an opportunity to make their positions clear.

The problems that most often arise during enactment are (a) overacting the role, (b) distorting the facts of the role, or (c) stepping out of the role.

Overacting comes most often when a player cops out of participating. In essence, the role-player is saying, "If I really exaggerate this, everyone will know that this is not the way I would act normally." If this occurs, the presenter should step in, ask the role-player what changes he or she could make to improve the approach, and assess the problem. Sometimes it is helpful to let the audience act as consultants, asking them what the problem is and what approach might be better. Usually the role-player will follow the direction the consultants set forth and can continue with the exercise.

Making up facts not in the role generally does not affect the overall results and can usually be left alone. Occasionally, however, the facts may undermine the basic purpose of the role-play. In that case, the presenter should stop the exercise for a moment and clarify some of the key facts. The role-player should be asked to review the key points and then the exercise can continue.

Stepping out of the role requires firm control by the presenter. Simply insist that the player keep in character by saying, "Don't tell us what you would do differently. Just act out the part as if your character were in this situation. Do whatever would be natural."

Step 5: Discussion

It is important to include the actors in the discussion, either as part of the audience, before the audience discussion, or as a follow-up to the audience discussion.

Discussion should be based on the characters and not the players. Character names should be used. All discussion should be focused on the facts, problems, and principals and not on an evaluation of the actors' performances. In many cases, it is best to let the actors discuss their feelings about their characters first. This can remove any hesitancy on the part of the audience to discuss certain roles.

In discussion, the presenter should ask questions such as, "What happened here?" "How could the situation have been changed?" and "What were the motives and feelings being acted out here?" The presenter should encourage the audience to reach beyond the role-play and suggest alternatives and other solutions, then decide on the best one.

Step 6: Evaluation

After the discussion, it is up to the presenter to pull together all the feelings and facts that have been presented and discussed. The evaluation period is the time to formulate conclusions or solutions to the situations presented. Brookfield recommends videotaping the role-play in order to provide an objective means of critical analysis by which the participants can compare and contrast successes and failures during an evaluation session.

Variations of Role-Playing

Within the two main types of role-playing, structured and spontaneous, there are three subtypes or variations. The variations can be used whether the type of role-play is structured or spontaneous, but they occur most often within the structured role-play. A true spontaneous role-playing situation obtains both the problem and the solution from the group, and material for the exercise is drawn from them.

The three variations are (a) single role-plays, (b) multiple role-plays, and (c) role rotation. These are addressed in more detail below.

Single Role-Plays

A single role-play is when two or three people act out roles in front of the group. It is then analyzed and discussed by all members of the group.

The single role-play is especially useful when demonstrating techniques or showing how certain problems can be dealt with.

Multiple Role-Plays

A multiple role-play involves the whole group as players. The group is broken into subgroups of two or three, and each player is given a written role or a set of characteristics around which to build his or her character. The entire class plays at the same time, and discussion is more effective if done in the small-group settings. Multiple role-plays are best used when the group needs practice in dealing with a specific problem or situation rather than changing attitudes or increasing personal insight.

Role Rotation

Role rotation consists of one person acting out a problem or situation, followed by several class members responding with solutions. Usually, the discussion can follow after three to five members have responded. It is similar to single role-plays but helps to alleviate some the of hesitation players may feel about acting out their roles.

Appropriate Uses,
Suggestions, and Cautions

Role-playing dramatizes situations. It is most commonly used for one of three very different goals: (a) training in specific sales techniques; (b) teaching skills such as interviewing, employee relations, or other people-centered activities; or (c) developing insight into human relations problems and emotions. Role-playing can best be used to

1. Discover how people might act under certain conditions
2. Gain insight into participants' own feelings and attitudes
3. Encourage understanding of others' feelings and attitudes
4. Illustrate different aspects of a human relations problem and open those aspects for discussion
5. Provide skills and practice in problem solving

Before choosing role-playing as the technique to use, the presenter should be sure of his or her objectives. By setting clear-cut targets, presenters are able to use role-playing to its fullest capabilities. If, for example, the objective is to improve skills, then the discussion following the role-playing should focus on how effectively the players used the skills in question.

An important point to watch in role-playing is to be certain that the discussion focuses on the character and not the player. By removing the player from the discussion and addressing the character, the risk of hurt feelings is considerably lessened.

In discussion, participants should be told to make their comments in relationship to their own feelings. Second-guessing should be discouraged. Focus on the role as it was played, not as someone else would have played it. *

Advantages, Disadvantages, and Limitations of Role-Playing

When using the role-playing instructional strategy, the presenter should be aware of the following advantages, disadvantages, and limitations of this technique.

Advantages of Role-Playing

1. Opportunity to practice and develop skills in a safe situation
2. Opportunity to analyze others' points of view and to express feelings and attitudes
3. Encourages active participation by entire group
4. Addresses behavior and emotions not easily presented in other means
5. High retention due to dramatic nature of presentation
6. Encourages participant to feel rather than intellectualize a situation
7. Provides means of presenting several solutions to a single problem
8. Encourages creativity and cooperation
9. Opportunity to learn to organize thoughts and responses quickly while reacting to a question or situation
10. Individualizes information to participants in a way that is understandable and familiar to them (Spain, 1992)

Disadvantages of Role-Playing

1. Some players may feel embarrassed.
2. If players do badly, presenter may have difficulty handling negative comments honestly without harming player.
3. It is time-consuming because it includes not only exercise but follow-up discussion and analysis.
4. It is ineffective if exercise runs too long.
5. It can sometimes be above the group's level of understanding.
6. It tends to overemphasize performance and neglect underlying purpose.
7. Participants with gregarious personalities or acting talent may monopolize the activity.

8. In structured role-playing, role sheets are difficult to design and write.
9. If participants fail to relate to situations, the exercise time is wasted.

Limitations of Role-Playing

1. Participants may be unable to identify realistically with the characters or behaviors.
2. It is not appropriate for large groups.
3. It must be kept within strict boundaries in order to meet objectives.
4. It can be viewed by some as "playing" and not taken seriously.
5. Controversial or highly emotional topics may get out of hand.
6. The method may be harmful to those who lack necessary skills to play (those who are shy or have a speech problem, for example).
7. It may benefit only role-players unless the objectives for the class are carefully specified.

Examples or Applications

Role-playing strategies can be applied in many situations, and some player characteristics will naturally arise in the situations. Topics such as a businessperson asking his or her boss for a raise, a teacher meeting with an irate parent, an atheist encountering an evangelist, or a White police officer harassing an African American can all be used for role-playing.

Within each role-playing exercise, different roles or types of characters can be presented (some players will be given or will assume more than one characteristic). Examples of some of these are

1. *Information giver* who contributes his or her beliefs and experiences
2. *Information seeker* who ask questions and brings out principles
3. *Initiator* who suggests new ideas or new problems
4. *Coordinator* who tries to bring the group together
5. *Orienter* who tries to get the group to define the goals
6. *Energizer* who motivates the group to productivity
7. *Summarizer* who pulls information together
8. *Encourager* who offers praise and acceptance
9. *Follower* who agrees with the majority of the group
10. *Aggressor* who attacks opinions of others
11. *Recognition seeker* who relates his own experiences
12. *Distractor* who interrupts discussion with horseplay or indifference
13. *Blocker* who is negative on all issues and resists the majority at all costs

Summary

Whether structured or spontaneous, role-playing can fill special purposes in the teaching structure. Waters, Woods, and Noel (1992) believe that the presenters play a key role in keeping the participants on task during the role-play, acting as a resource if questions arise, and helping the participants review and study the worth of their actions during role-play. It is helpful in leading participants to better understand their own behavior and the behavior of others. In addition, if properly used and carefully prepared, it can stimulate interesting and thoughtful discussion.

References

Brookfield, S. D. (1990). *The skillful teacher.* San Francisco: Jossey-Bass.

Joyce, B., Weil, M., & Showers, B. (1992). *Models of teaching.* Boston: Allyn & Bacon.

Span, R. (1992). Role play and reactions: Identifying with the elements. *The Science Teacher, 59*(9), 38-40.

Swink, D. F. (1993). Role-play your way to learning. *Training and Development, 47*(5), 91-97.

Waters, E., Woods, P., & Noel, S. (1992). Role play: A versatile cooperative learning activity. *Contemporary Education, 63*(3), 216-218.

The Role-Playing Planning Sheet

Date:_____Time:_____Site:_____

Purpose of the Session:

Relationship to Former/Future Learning:

Objective(s) of Session:

Warm-up Activity:

Directions for Warm-up:

      1.
      2.
      3.
      4.
      5.

Situations for Role-Play:

Directions for Role-Players:

Directions to Other Participants:

Discussion Questions (to follow each role-play):

Handouts (for role-players and other participants)

Summary Notes:

The Role-Playing Evaluation Sheet

(⚫You may wish to have someone else consider these items,
as well as evaluating yourself.)

⚫How well did the stated purpose relate to former/future learning?

How well did the purpose relate to the role-play situations?

⚫Were directions for the warm-up clear and logical?
    __Yes __No (Explain)

⚫Did the warm-up "set the mood" for the rest of the session?
    __Yes __No (Explain)

⚫Were the directions to players clear? __Yes   __No (Explain)

⚫Were the directions to other participants clear? __Yes __No (Explain)

What did the facilitator do to alleviate any tension regarding role-playing?

Were the players realistic in their roles? __Yes __No (Explain)

Was there a helpful discussion of each situation? __Yes __No (Explain)

⚫Were the handouts helpful? __Yes __No (Explain)

⚫Did the facilitor effectively summarize and bring closure to the session? __Yes __No (Explain)

⚫What was most effective about this session?

⚫Suggestions for improvement:

4
Case Study

Definition

The case study learning method uses real or hypothetical situations, circumstances, and problems to help participants understand and practice problem solving. The situation, or case, can be either written or on film and must contain sufficient detail and data.

Introduction

The case study is a study of firsthand experiences contributed by participants, actual cases pulled by the teacher, or hypothetical cases designed to point out specific problem areas or personality types.

The study of the case is designed to help participants understand and practice problem-solving and decision-making approaches. Relevant details are studied and examined by the students, who then analyze and discuss the problem.

Main Procedural Steps in Using the Case Study

In the case study method, the process may be done by the group as a whole or by smaller subgroups. To begin, the leader or teacher must explain specific guidelines, set objectives, and present a precise means of evaluation. The case should be relevant to the students and usually involves some kind of conflict.

The cases themselves may be presented in one of three ways:

1. The cases may be actual experiences that members of the group have had. In that case, the presenter or leader needs to be sure that the participant relating the experience presents sufficient data for the situation to be reviewed.
2. The case may be a written case, either factual or hypothetical, that the presenter presents to the group.
3. The case may be presented by a film or movie. For complicated cases, films and movies are especially helpful because the personalities of the participants can be seen by the class.

A good case or incident should be genuinely interesting and pertinent, be somewhat controversial or at least be open to a difference of opinion, and present events and objective facts from several members of the group. The participants can be given no more information than what the person in the situation had. Proposed solutions should contribute to the overall growth of the participants.

Once the case has been presented, the group identifies and interprets the information as it has been presented. The group then analyzes the data and evaluates the nature of the problem. Whenever possible, data should be objective, with no value judgments prescribed. Analysis of the data is usually by means of reference materials or textbooks but can also include personal interviews, group interviews, or field study.

Participants are invited to share personal feelings and attitudes about the problem, study and evaluate the data, and then make decisions or formulate a plan of action.

Christensen (1987) notes that case studies integrate inductive and deductive thinking on the part of the participant to sort through various options, remedy a particular problem, and find the most successful solution.

In some cases, a leader and recorder may be needed for each group. When using small groups, each group will report. After each group has contributed its ideas, the whole class makes a decision. Sometimes the decision will be oral and sometimes written.

During the discussion phase, the presenter or leader needs to make sure that the participants are moving in the right direction.

Whether oral or written, the following five steps should be taken.

1. Identify the true problem.
2. Choose the important facts to be considered with the problem.
3. List several possible solutions.
4. Evaluate the results of each solution.
5. Determine which one solution is best.

Variations of the
Case Study

The case study has few variations, except in the division of the group. A large group can be divided into smaller groups who study the problem independently. The class can study the case as a whole, or the cases can be studied and solved on an individual basis.

In addition, the time period that is used to discuss the case and arrive at a decision can range from a portion of a class period to the whole period, or to an entire semester or year.

When time permits, other learning strategies such as role-playing, simulation, the interview, and questioning can be used effectively with the case study method.

Appropriate Uses,
Suggestions, and Cautions

The case study method is commonly used when the subjects under consideration fall into one of the following categories:

- ✓ Human relations
- ✓ Job interviews
- ✓ Salesmanship, particularly with experienced salespeople
- ✓ Supervisory training
- ✓ Business organizational situations
- ✓ Distribution economics

In addition, the method can be effectively used for any subject of study in which issues are discussed or opinions are apt to be divided.

The case study method is best for finding solutions to a wide variety of problems and situations. It is not effective when searching for abstract principles. When the participants do not have real experiences to draw on to illustrate the points under study, then case studies can provide an excellent frame of reference. Ryan (1994) insists that the case acts as a catalyst that encourages the participants to play the roles of the characters in a certain situation, allowing them to problem solve from a personal, realistic perspective. It encourages discussion and is good for getting an entire group focused on a specific problem.

The case study technique provides a good forum for exchanging ideas about real-life problems that the students may actually face in the world of work. In doing so, it helps bridge the gap between classroom and real life.

Caution is necessary because the method depends on well-prepared cases and an effective discussion leader. Often, especially when dealing with complex situations, the students need to be experienced in handling real-life situations. When presenting the case to be studied, the situation must be clearly and adequately presented with enough details to enable the students to get a clear picture of the situation. Owenby (1992) is convinced that case studies must be descriptive, in the form of a story, sequential in order, and realistic for participants to approach them eagerly.

The method requires students to deduce the principles involved, make decisions, and predict results. Maturity of the participants is often an issue in deciding when to use the case study method.

Advantages, Disadvantages, and Limitations of the Case Study

When using the case study instructional strategy, the teacher should be aware of the following advantages, disadvantages, and limitations of this technique.

Advantages of the Case Study

1. Interest and motivation of participants is generally high.
2. There is better retention of content due to active student involvement.
3. It develops responsibility on the part of the participants.
4. Conclusions are made based on the participants' problem-solving skills. Practice sharpens those skills.
5. Realistic cases bridge the gap between school and the real world.
6. The leader can present a problem in a minimum amount of time, especially if film or other audiovisuals are used to present the case.
7. Boyce, King, and Harris (1993) state that case studies encourage participants to positively critique peer ideas and work cooperatively in a group.

Disadvantages of the Case Study

1. It is time-consuming.
2. Good case studies that participants can relate to are hard to find.
3. The procedure is often unmanageable for normal classroom size.

4. Teacher must be well prepared for the topic of study.
5. Students may come to believe that all complex problems have simple solutions, based on case study experiences.
6. Cases developed by participants may be controversial and difficult for teacher to handle.
7. The problem may seem irrelevant to some class members.

Limitations of the Case Study

1. It is most effective when used with mature participants.
2. Resources and materials needed to study cases may not be readily available.
3. Evaluation is difficult due to the open-discussion format of the cases.
4. Cases presented for discussion must be within the experience range of the group.
5. If cases are not presented clearly and with sufficient data, participants may get sidetracked into reading conditions into the case.

Examples or Applications

Case studies may be factual or fictitious. The experiences can be those of the teacher, a student, or another person. Sometimes the participants will want to diagnose the causes of a problem, rather than search for a solution. Other times, the solution is the goal, and the discussion should be geared toward making decisions.

The case study can also be applied simply for an exchange of ideas among the participants, rather than searching for a textbook-type answer.

When the case study is properly directed, the strategy can be used to reach decisions about school or community problems.

Summary

Case studies are based on data and research while drawing from real-life situations. They provide high retention of ideas and high levels of motivation for the participants, especially when the case is one that they can relate to. Case studies provide active participation on the part of students. Stolovich (1990) praises the case study method as an activity that sharpens problem-solving skills. The presenter, once the case is carefully chosen, can also use a wide range of other teaching methods to complement the case study discipline.

References

Boyce, A., King, V., & Harris, B. (1993, March 24-28). *The case study approach for pedagogists.* Paper presented at the annual meeting of the American Alliance for Health, Physical Education, Recreation and Dance, Washington, D.C.

Christensen, C. R. (1987). *Teaching and the case method.* Boston: Harvard Business School Press.

Owenby, P. H. (1992). Making case studies come alive. *Training, 29*(1), 43-46.

Ryan, C. W. (1994, May 21). *Case studies in teacher education: A series for working with students at risk.* Paper presented at Central State University, Wilberforce, Ohio.

Stolovitch, H. (1990). Case study method. *Performance and Instruction, 29*(9), 35-37.

The Case Study Planning Sheet

Date:_____Time:_____Site:_____

Purpose of the Case Study:

Relationship to Former/Future Learning:

Objective(s) of Session:

By Which Method Will the Case Study Be Presented?

1. Actual experiences that members of the group have had
2. A written case, either factual or hypothetical
3. Case presented by a film or movie

Steps to Take to Carry Out a Case Study:

1. Identify the true problem.
2. Choose the important facts to be considered with the problem.
3. List several possible solutions.
4. Evaluate the results of each solution.
5. Determine which one solution is best.

Discussion Questions (to follow case study):

Handouts (concerning case study and other information relating to the case):

Summary Notes:

The Case Study Evaluation Sheet

(⏏You may wish to have someone else consider these items,
as well as evaluating yourself.)

⏏How well did the stated purpose relate to former/future
learning?

Was the case study appropriate for the topic?
__Yes __No (Explain)

⏏ Was the method by which the case study was presented
appropriate? __Yes __No (Explain)

⏏Were time allocations suitable? __Yes __No (Explain)

⏏Were the directions clear and logical? __Yes __No (Explain)

⏏Were the directions to other participants clear?
__Yes __No (Explain)

What did the facilitator do to alleviate any tension regarding
the case study?

Were the discussion questions that followed the case study
appropriate? __Yes __No (Explain)

⏏Were the handouts helpful in presenting the case study?
__Yes __No (Explain)

⏏ Did the facilitor effectively summarize and bring closure to
the session? __Yes __No (Explain)

⏏What was most effective about this session?

⏏Suggestions for improvement:

5

Demonstration

Definition

Demonstration is a teaching method that presenters use to visually teach and explain a sequential process or facts and concepts. It requires manipulation on the part of the presenter and observation on the part of the participant. Participants are able to see how to do a particular task or solve a problem by watching the presenter and listening to verbal, step-by-step explanations that guide the participants to imitate them later on their own.

Introduction

Effective presenters want to teach dynamic material that is of interest to the participants. Teaching methods need to be tailored to the needs of the participants. Participants learn in a variety of ways, and many are visual learners who require a hands-on teaching method. Some ideas are difficult to explain and need to be demonstrated to participants in order to be understood. The demonstration method allows the participant to see the sequence of steps and hear a verbal explanation of how each is performed. The United Nations Educational, Scientific, and Cultural Organization (1985) says that demonstrations develop synchronized cognitive and motor skills, sensory development, and logical thought patterns.

Main Procedural Steps in Using the Demonstration

The four basic steps of a demonstration are preparation, presentation, application, and testing and follow-up.

Step 1: Preparation

The presenter should prepare all the information, tools, supplies, and equipment before the demonstration takes place. Everything must be accessible and ready to operate at a certain time for the demonstration to be effective. The size of the materials should be taken into account to allow for ample room and should not cause overcrowding or awkward use.

The presenter must be sure that an appropriate place has been chosen for the demonstration. The participants should be arranged so all can see and hear. The semicircle and series of rows facing the presenter are good seating arrangements. The presenter should arrange the participants in such a way to prevent inattention, obstruction, and boredom.

The demonstration should be physically or mentally rehearsed to check for mistakes and create continuity of ideas. Clermont, Borko, and Krajcik (1994) find that presenters with an extensive knowledge base of their subject area and familiarity with their audiences experience the greatest success when using the demonstration as a teaching method. They state that these experienced presenters are able to field questions better and provide mental representations more easily than novices.

There should be a written plan to follow as a guideline. It should be given to the participants when they are ready to learn this content. The demonstration should be planned around the size of the class and vary in length accordingly.

Step 2: Presentation

The presentation allows the presenter to describe the different steps, proper procedures, and main ideas of the skill while actually doing them. Basic vocabulary, short sentences, and familiar words should be used to maintain the attention and understanding of the participants.

The presentation should follow an outline to be sure all the steps are accounted for. Present the information sparingly, one point at a time, to ensure understanding. The presenter should present the information in sequential steps, working from the most basic to the more difficult, paced by the understanding of the participants. The information should be closely related to the steps being performed and be kept to a minimum with no deviations in thought. There are many ways to do something, but the participants should be taught a specific method, and it should be learned thoroughly before another is attempted.

The demonstration should begin by finding out what knowledge participants already have and relating the new knowledge to that. The demonstration should follow soon after to let the participants know that they too will have a chance to participate. The participants will be more interested in the lesson if they know they will have the chance to use the same equipment or apply what they have learned on their own in their own way.

Step 3: Application

Application allows the participant to practice what he or she has heard and seen from the presenter's demonstration. A presenter is close by to monitor the participants' decisions and actions. The participants are able to practice their listening and manual skills as they perform the demonstration while the presenter calls out each step. This provides a chance for the participants to mimic the presenter's previous actions but do the work on their own.

It is important not to take over through suggestions or criticism and remove the participant's sense of importance or responsibility to his or her demonstration. The presenter should point out errors and help the participant think of ways to correct the mistake, then let the participant fix it. Daines (1993) says that it is important to encourage confidence in the participants so they won't be so hesitant to participate or perform the demonstration on their own, and so they will realize that mistakes will be made and can be corrected.

Step 4: Testing and Follow-up

The testing step shows whether or not the participant has understood and mastered the aims of the demonstration to the presenter's satisfaction. Each participant must execute and accomplish the skill the presenter sets before him or her individually. The participant learns for himself or herself the satisfaction and self-confidence of mastering a skill through learning by doing. The testing step is not a time for presenters to offer help but to observe the participant's actions and help only if there is an emergency. The participant must meet the standards and goals the presenter places before him or her in order to have mastered the skill.

Variations of the Demonstration

A variation of the standard demonstration process is allowing participant involvement within the demonstration. First, the presenter does the demonstration and explains what is happening. Then a participant performs the same operation while the presenter explains. Then another participant performs the demonstration and tells what is happening. When the participants are directly involved, they learn more. With the participant involvement, the presenter is provided with immediate feedback about the success or failure of the demonstration.

Another variation is the use of an assistant to aid the presenter in the demonstration. It could be another presenter or an advanced participant. Having someone who is skilled in this area of the demonstration adds practicality and variety.

Penick (1993) suggests a variation on the standard demonstration technique in which the participants are given a 1-minute demonstration of a particularly tricky experiment. Then they are given the materials and told to figure out how to reenact the demonstration to have the same results as the professor. Penick adds that this variation is mainly useful for stimulating creative thought.

Appropriate Uses, Suggestions, and Cautions

Many times, specific information like manipulative skills and scientific theories are presented in step-by-step processes to ensure understanding and applicability. Demonstration allows participants to show what they have learned and gain an understanding all of the information behind the skill and the reasons for actually applying the skill. Application of the skill leads to practice and eventual mastery. The sequential steps help teach participants logical thought patterns when applying a skill or attacking a problem.

The demonstration is used mostly for teaching scientific principles, the movement and relationship of parts of equipment, and hands-on skills. It is also used in math, mechanics, practical arts, and vocational and technical education. But it is helpful in any instructional setting when a presenter wants to show participants how to do something.

The participants must try not to fall behind or get lost during the demonstration because a missed step might leave participants confused with no way to catch up. The demonstration must be interesting and have some relevance to the participants for them to stay attentive.

Advantages, Disadvantages, and Limitations of the Demonstration

When using the demonstration instructional strategy, the presenter should be aware of the following advantages, disadvantages, and limitations of this technique.

Advantages of Demonstration

1. It is a hands-on method of learning.
2. It is very effective for visual learners.
3. It is a good way to teach vocational or industrial trades.
4. It teaches participants to think sequentially.
5. Participants are directly involved in their learning.

Disadvantages of Demonstration

1. Without proper planning or preparation, it is ineffective.
2. Key steps may be skipped, leaving participants confused.
3. The length or complexity of the demonstration may lead to boredom and confusion.
4. Participants might be distracted by the materials.
5. Slow learners may feel in the "spotlight" and not participate.

Limitations of Demonstration

1. Equipment and materials may not always be available.
2. The demonstration must be timely in terms of participant readiness and relevance to other lessons.
3. The presenter may talk to the materials, not to the participants.
4. Sometimes real materials are too costly and substitutes must be used.

Examples or Applications

Demonstrations can take many forms. Each method should be appropriate to both the needs of the participant and the objective of the presenter. For example, if the class needs specific instruction in a particular area of electronics, a chalkboard illustration may suffice. An illustrated lecture might correctly address new developments or provide an overview of a particular subject. Texts provide detailed information and drawings on a number of technical and advanced subjects. Also, a sports skill might be properly demonstrated by a coach with a basketball. Each subject determines which method works best.

Summary

The demonstration is a rewarding teaching method because after close observation of the presenter, the participants are able to model the procedure they just witnessed and understand the information surrounding the demonstration. The participants are able to perform the skill afterward, so they learn how and the reasons why. Demonstration provides a stimulating hands-on approach to learning that provides the participant with a sense of applicability and practicality. Hugo (1993) believes that when participants view demonstrations as relevant in some way to them, they are motivated to experience and store the demonstration for future learning or use.

References

Clermont, C., Borko, H., & Krajcik, J. (1994). Comparative study of the pedagogical content knowledge of experienced and novice chemical demonstrators. *Journal of Research in Science Teaching, 31*(4), 419-439.

Daines, J. (1993). *Adult learning, adult teaching.* Nottingham, England: Nottingham University, Department of Adult Education. (ERIC Document Reproduction Service No. ED 361 597)

Hugo, J. (1993). Combining gases in classes. *Science Teacher, 60*(2), 26-29.

Penick, J. (1993). The mysterious closed system. *Science Teacher, 60*(2), 30-33.

United Nations Educational, Scientific and Cultural Organization, Division of Science, Technical and Environmental Education. (1985). *A problem-solving approach to environmental education.* Environmental Education Series. Paris: Author. (ERIC Document Reproduction Service No. ED 354 143)

The Demonstration Planning Sheet

Date:_____Time:_____Site:_____

Anticipated Size of Audience:

Title of the Demonstration:

Objective(s) of Session:

Rehearsal Notes:

Relationship to Former Learning:

Demonstration

1. Introduction
2. Procedural steps
3. Statement of results
4. Check for understanding
5. Volunteer demonstration
6. Check for understanding
7. Other demonstration practices (if this is planned)

Handouts:

Equipment Needs:

Plan for Group Practice (if any):

Summary Notes and Follow-up (assignment or preview):

The Demonstration
Evaluation Sheet

(❤You may wish to have someone else consider these items,
as well as evaluating yourself.)

❤Was the purpose clearly stated? __Yes __No (Explain)

Did the presenter ascertain and build on participants' prior
knowledge? __Yes __No (Explain)

❤Were vocabulary words and terms effectively explained?
__Yes __No (Explain)

Was the demonstation appropriate for the purpose?
__Yes __No (Explain)

❤Did the presenter pace the demonstration for full understanding of the purpose and the procedure? __Yes __No (Explain)

How effective was this check for understanding?

❤If there was a volunteer demonstration, did this flow well?
__Yes __No (Explain)

❤Was the presenter supportive so that the volunteer appeared
successful? __Yes __No (Explain)

Did the volunteer demonstration serve as a good review of the
purpose and the procedure? __Yes __No (Explain)

If others were able to try the demonstration, was this preceded
by a check for understanding? __Yes __No (Explain)

Did most participants appear to understand the procedure and
the presenter's expectations before beginning this phase of the
session? __Yes __No (Explain)

❤How effective was the monitoring of individual work?

❤How helpful were the handouts?

Were equipment and other materials adequate?
__Yes __No (Explain)

❤What was the most effective aspect of the session?

❤Suggestions for improvement:

6

Panel

Definition

A panel is a discussion by a small group of persons, usually three to eight, who present brief lectures on a topic about which they have special knowledge. The discussion takes place in the presence of an audience and with the help of a moderator who oversees the discussion. Litecky (1992) believes that the panel presentation is an active exercise that presents the participant with the opportunity to practice and be confident in oral presentation and individual thinking.

Introduction

The panel, or panel discussion, may be formal or informal, depending on the participation of the audience. Although the presentation may be conversational and have a high level of audience participation, it is a purposeful discussion wherein varying positions and points of view will be presented.

Main Procedural Steps
in Using the Panel

Setting the stage for a panel is a simple task, but planning can be important to the overall success. The panel should not be too far away from the audience, especially if the discussion is to be more informal. Panel members should sit behind a table, facing the audience. It is more effective if the panel sits on a platform or stage so that it is raised above the audience. If the audience is large, microphones should be used.

The moderator of the panel is responsible for keeping the discussion moving in the right direction, pulling out points of interest from the panel members' lectures, and making sure that all members have a chance to participate equally.

A skillful panel moderator is able to avoid the biggest pitfalls of panel discussions: Keeping the panel members on the topic, and clarifying statements made by the panel.

In the panel discussion, each member of the panel makes statements or presents his or her position. Each panel member is given the same amount of time, and it is up to the panel moderator to keep the speakers within their allotted time frame. After each panel member has been allowed to speak, the moderator asks for contributions from the audience, in the form of either questions or comments.

Usually the time is divided in half, with 20 or 30 minutes allotted to the panel lectures and an equal amount of time dedicated to audience questions and comments.

The moderator should meet with panel members in advance of the discussion and introduce panel members to the group at the beginning of the discussion. The teacher may assign time limits, but the moderator should announce the schedule and explain all procedures to the group.

Finally, the moderator opens the panel discussion with a question designed to arouse interest. Following the discussion, the moderator will ask questions to clarify statements and work to maintain the theme of the discussion.

Variations of the Panel

The panel forum is the only variation of this technique. The pure panel discussion allows for no audience participation. The panel members discuss the subject among themselves, with the moderator preparing questions in advance and adding questions to keep the discussion alive.

The panel forum is a panel discussion that is followed by audience participation in a free and open discussion. Hungerford (1989) says the panel presentation method provides an active learning atmosphere in which participants are encouraged to share their personal opinions and ideologies with others, thus creating a free flow of ideas. The moderator acts as a buffer between the panel and the audience. Sometimes questions are submitted in advance by audience members and read to the panel by the moderator.

Appropriate Uses, Suggestions, and Cautions

The panel discussion or panel forum depends on interesting topics, panelists who are well informed, and a skillful moderator to keep things moving. It is similar to the lecture except that the panelists can present differing points of view.

The panel discussion is appropriate for introducing new materials, motivating students, and summarizing an area of study. It is especially helpful when the participants are divided on an issue or have differing opinions. Dienstfrey (1991) suggests using the panel discussion in the form of a game. For instance, the participants become Shakespearean characters from a novel, and the class must probe them for information about themselves, thus stimulating the students to learn in a creative, fun way.

Often a panel is used when a group is too large to be divided into small groups. It is also a convenient technique when the discussion of a problem as a whole is too broad in scope. The panel discussion encourages a high level of interaction, especially if the group is involved in the selection of topics. According to the *Instructional Improvement Handbook* (Instructional Improvement Committee, 1982), the panel discussion is also helpful when it involves an outside speaker or panel of speakers who can contribute their knowledge and expertise to spark questions and curiosity from the class.

Advantages, Disadvantages, and Limitations of the Panel

When using the panel instructional strategy, the teacher should be aware of the following advantages, disadvantages, and limitations of this technique.

Advantages of the Panel

1. A number of different views on a topic may be presented.
2. Panel members enjoy a high level of freedom to express views or thoughts.
3. Informality can be maintained, allowing for good communication.
4. Different sides of complicated issues can be presented to a large number of people.

Disadvantages of the Panel

1. Panel members frequently fail to keep on the topic.
2. One panel member may monopolize the subject, regardless of whether or not his or her knowledge is as broad as the other panel members.
3. The audience can become confused by poor panel presentations.
4. If the presentation is not systematic, questions may be left unanswered.

Limitations of the Panel

1. It is difficult to find six to eight panel members who are not only skillful in discussion but also have a strong knowledge of the subject to be discussed.
2. The panel discussion must be carefully planned, but it may be difficult to get panel members together prior to discussion.

Examples or Applications

The panel discussion is most similar to the lecture, except that it offers different points of view. It is best applied to stimulate interest in a topic and to identify and clarify problems or issues.

Any topic that can stimulate discussion can be used for a panel discussion. It is good for bringing several points of view before the group and promoting understanding of the different parts of a topic. According to Jensen (1989), panel discussions that are centered around up-to-date issues and questions based on values and beliefs will help build a more effective and culturally literate society.

Summary

The panel or panel discussion involves both the audience and a group of people who have a special knowledge about a topic. In the classroom, the panel members can be assigned different points of the topic for discussion or can express their own opinions on controversial and emotional issues.

The panel has the benefits of the lecture in that a large amount of material can be presented quickly to a large group, but it overcomes the lecture's lack of participation by involving the audience.

References

Dienstfrey, S. (1991). *Creative approaches to teaching Shakespeare in high school.* (ERIC Document Reproduction Service No. ED 331 096)

Hungerford, H. (1989). *A prototype environmental education curriculum for the middle school. A discussion guide for the Unesco training seminars on environmental education* (Environmental Education Series 29). Paris: United Nations Educational, Scientific and Cultural Organization, Division of Science, Technical and Environmental Education. (ERIC Document Reproduction Service No. ED 326 420)

Instructional Improvement Committee. (1992). *Instructional improvement handbook.* Wisconsin University, Paper Identified by the Task Force on Establishing a National Clearinghouse of Materials Developed for Teaching Assistant Training. (ERIC Document Reproduction Service No. ED 285 495)

Jensen, M. (1989). *Increasing cultural literacy in the basic speech communication course.* (ERIC Document Reproduction Service No. ED 302 860)

Litecky, L. (1992). Great teaching, great learning: Classroom climate, innovative methods and critical thinking. *New Directions for Community Colleges, 20*(1), 83-90.

The Panel Planning Sheet

Date:_____Time:_____Site:_____

Intended Audience:

Topic Statement Question:

Objective(s) of the Panel:

Arrangements:

      Set-up, Furnishings, Audiovisuals:

      Secure Panel Members and Moderator:

      Assist With Travel Arrangements:

Publicity:

Presession Meeting:

Introduction of Panel Members to Audience:

Procedure of Session:

Questions From Audience (if this is to be included):

Summary Notes:

Postsession Plans (thank you, etc.):

The Panel Evaluation Sheet

(You may wish to have someone else consider these items,
as well as evaluating yourself.)

Was the topic/question well stated? __Yes __No (Explain)

Was the publicity appropriate, timely, adequate?
    __Yes __No (Explain)

Did travel arrangements run smoothly for all panel members
    and the moderator? __Yes __No (Explain)

Were site arrangements adequate? __Yes __No (Explain)

Did the presession contribute to the overall effectiveness of
    the session? __Yes __No (Explain)

Was the moderator effective in keeping the discussion on
    track? . . . in developing cohesiveness? . . . in clarifying?
        __Yes __No (Explain)

What was the quality of panel members' contributions to the
    discussion?

Did the summary bring effective closure to the session?
        __Yes __No (Explain)

How responsive was the audience?

Was there audience participation in the form of questions or
comments? __Yes __No If so, how did that contribute to the
overall effectiveness of the session?

Which aspect of the session was best?

Suggestions for improvement:

7

Inquiry Method

Definition

The inquiry method is a type of questioning technique that involves questioning by the participants, not necessarily to find a single factual answer but to solve physical, behavioral, philosophical, and historical problems. It uses the what, why, and how of teaching.

Introduction

With the inquiry method, participants are encouraged to use a scientific approach and then interpret the results to form their answers or opinions. Inquiry is concerned with problem solving, but it does not require solutions. The approach toward solving the problem is systematic yet flexible, and often there is no one correct answer. Henson (1993) supports the inquiry method because it shuns one correct answer in favor of many ideas and removes fear of failure on the part of the participant when contributing to the exercise.

Inquiry is frequently used in science and math, where participants are "rediscovering" the answer to the problem. The method is, however, relevant for most other subjects, including those that address questions of philosophy and behavior that may have no one correct answer.

Main Procedural Steps in
Using the Inquiry Method

The inquiry method requires that presenters have expertise not only in the subject matter being discussed but also in the teaching strategy itself. There are some pitfalls to inquiry, and this expertise is necessary to avoid them.

In implementing the inquiry method, the teacher creates the situation, whether it be physical or psychological. Scientific laws and laws of nature are good examples of physical problems where the truth can be rediscovered with the inquiry method. Problems of ethics and decisions in which individual prejudices become an issue are good philosophical problems for inquiry.

Once the problem is presented, the presenter then acts simply as a facilitator. In solving the problem, the participant uses raw data and discipline to address the problem. Once the presenter has set the stage, he or she acts as a type of structural referee and should refrain from commenting on the direction the discussion is going.

When the participants have gained enough information to develop a hypothesis, the presenter may provide some additional information that challenges that hypothesis, thereby not allowing any answer to be absolute or final.

When the inquiry discussion is over, the teacher should lead the group in reviewing and evaluating the experience, because the process involved is as much a learning experience as the answers given. Bellon, Bellon, and Blank (1992) state that presenters should ask questions that are open-ended and exploratory in order to stimulate the participants to examine all their options. Participants should be able to share their discoveries, including what aspects of the discussion made them uncomfortable, what turned them off to the whole issue, and whether or not they felt in tune with the group.

Inquiry should be used only when the leader has enough expertise in the subject matter to handle unexpected "discoveries." Setting up the discovery requires detailed and thorough planning, as well as being sure that proper materials, information, and raw data are available.

Inquiry is a method in which the students find the answer themselves. Presenters should be prepared to accept their answers. Wolf (1993) believes participants are able to contribute more critical-thinking skills and gain more from the learning experience when the atmosphere is one that is more participant oriented and less presenter directed.

Variations of the Inquiry Method

In pure inquiry, there is no correct answer. The technique was originated by Socrates and is a highly personal experience in learning, even though it is usually approached with a group.

The interesting feature of inquiry as opposed to most other techniques is that it is a dual learning process. While the participants learn about the topic under investigation, they are also learning about the process of inquiry. The attitude of the learner is important because inquiry is a self-motivated technique.

Appropriate Uses, Suggestions, and Cautions

The inquiry method is appropriate to use both with physical problems, such as scientific or mathematical problems, and with behavioral and philosophical problems. Because there is no single answer, inquiry is a strong motivational learning style.

The inquiry method should be used only when cooperation is one of the goals. It fosters cooperation instead of competition. Presenters find they are more participant oriented instead of subject oriented.

The technique can be enhanced by using small groups within larger ones. It is a form of simulation. Participants use the data, accept or reject the opinions of others, and arrive at a conclusion collectively.

Advantages, Disadvantages, and Limitations of the Inquiry Method

When using the inquiry method instructional strategy, the teacher should be aware of the following advantages, disadvantages, and limitations of this technique.

Advantages of the Inquiry Method

1. Participants are actively discovering information, therefore retention is high.

2. Participants learn how to follow leads and clues and record findings.
3. Motivation comes from within. Participants are intrinsically motivated.
4. It encourages individual and creative thinking.
5. It encourages intuitive thinking.
6. It enables students to discover relationships and cause-and-effect variables.
7. It is highly participatory.

Disadvantages of the Inquiry Method

1. The technique is very time-consuming.
2. There is lack of textbooks and materials available for presenters.
3. Participants often get bogged down and lose direction before the problem is solved.
4. Participants often discover things other than what was intended to be discovered.
5. An erroneous discovery after great study and effort can be deflating for participants.
6. Presenters must have a strong background in the subject in order to handle unexpected discoveries.

Limitations of the Inquiry Method

1. Setting up the problem and conditions requires thorough planning.
2. Proper raw materials and data must be available.
3. Participants' skill level and maturity must be on a level with course objective and subject.
4. It does not stress accumulation of facts.
5. It is best when used with small or medium groups.
6. Cooper (1990) notes that the inquiry method is a highly subjective activity resulting in bias.

Examples or Applications

The inquiry method can be used in science or philosophy. Groups may be asked to study, for example, the heat conductivity in different types of pans by actually conducting experiments and arriving at a conclusion.

Another approach would be to set up a simulation of an ethical question and then get the group to arrive at a conclusion. An example might be a hospital advisory board that has to decide life-or-death questions concerning several different patients.

In inquiry, the presenter provides the materials and the situations and the participants provide the answers or possibilities. Joyce, Weil, and Showers (1992) state that the inquiry method is most successful in promoting critical thinking within an instructional atmosphere when the topic is challenging and somewhat confusing.

Summary

Inquiry is a high-retention, self-motivational style of learning that asks participants not to find the answer that the teacher has in mind but to arrive at their own conclusions and discoveries. It can be used with scientific questions or with emotional and philosophical questions. In some pure forms of inquiry, the assumption is that there is no "right" answer.

References

Bellon, J., Bellon, E., & Blank, M. (1992). *Teaching from a research knowledge base*. New York: Merrill.

Cooper, J. M. (1990). *Classroom teaching skills*. Toronto: D. C. Heath.

Henson, K. T. (1993). *Methods and strategies for teaching in secondary and middle schools*. New York: Longman.

Joyce, B., Weil, M., & Showers, B. (1992). *Models of teaching*. Boston: Allyn & Bacon.

Wolf, A. (1993). Project directors learn too. *Social Studies Review, 32*(3), 48-52.

The Inquiry Method
Planning Sheet

Date:_____Time:_____Site:_____

Problem Statement:

Objective(s) of Session:

Possible Options:

    1.
    2.
    3.

Resources Needed:

Handouts (background information, process sheet, etc.):

Follow-up Activity(ies):

Summary Notes (review and evaluation of findings):

The Inquiry Method
Evaluation Sheet

(You may wish to have someone else consider these items,
as well as evaluating yourself.)

Was the problem/situation well stated?
__Yes __No (Explain)

How well prepared were the participants for this session?

Was the facilitator nonbiased? __Yes __No (Explain)

Was the inquiry process clearly explained?
__Yes__No (Explain)

How effective was the facilitator in keeping participants
focused and moving forward?

What was the level of enthusiasm . . . of the facilitator? . . . of
the inquirers?

How effective were the handouts?

Were adequate resources available? __Yes __No (Explain)

Were site arrangements adequate? __Yes __No (Explain)

Was time allocation appropriate? __Yes __No (Explain)

How effectively did the participants use the inquiry process to
form and defend a hypothesis?

How well did the facilitator direct the inquiry process? (Was
he or she helpful without being directive?)

Was summarizing effective in bringing closure and clarifying
questions? __Yes __No (Explain)

What was best about this learning session?

Suggestions for improvement:

8

Buzz Groups

Definition

Buzz groups are formed by dividing large groups into small discussion groups of 2 to 15 people who meet simultaneously for a specified time to discuss a specific question, problem, or issue. Bellon, Bellon, and Blank (1992) note that such groups allow for an environment that fosters independent, cognitive thinking among group members with less reliance on presenter-based rote memorization.

Introduction

Buzz groups encourage more efficient discussion. They can be used in many different ways and are most often used in combination with other techniques, such as a lecture. Buzz groups set the groundwork to get discussion started. They are most often used when dealing with controversial subjects or difficult questions and problems.

Main Procedural Steps in Using the Buzz Group

Any size group can be divided into buzz groups if there is room available for the groups to get together. The leader begins by dividing the overall group into smaller groups of anywhere from 2 to

15 people. These smaller buzz groups should have room to sit either facing each other or in a circle, which will increase the discussion.

Once the groups are formed, the leader will introduce the issue or problem to be discussed. The issue can be the same for all groups, or each group can have a different phase or subproblem to discuss. The Professional Teacher Education Module Series (1984) suggests narrowing the topic, allowing for participant achievement level, and having time restrictions to prevent a high frustration level among the participants.

Once the issue or problem to be discussed is clarified and understood by each group, the groups should be asked to choose their own leaders and recorders, or the presenter can appoint one for each group.

The group leader makes certain that the members of the group become acquainted with each other, leads the discussion, and tries to get all the members of the group to participate. Williams (1983) offers that buzz groups provide participants with an interactive atmosphere that creates willing participation within a small or large group. The recorder takes notes and prepares a summary to be presented when all the groups come together.

When the buzz groups are very small, with only two or three members, the formality of selecting a group leader and recorder is not necessary. In those cases, the presenter should just ask each group to appoint a spokesperson to present their information at the end of the buzz group session.

The time allowed in the buzz groups should be specified at the beginning and can range anywhere from 2 to 20 minutes, depending on the number of people in each group, the complexity of the issue, and the purpose of the buzz groups. If the buzz groups are mainly designed to help the members get acquainted, for example, then the time needs to be short. If the groups are tackling a difficult problem or subproblem, then more time will be necessary.

While the groups are meeting, the teacher can move from group to group, listening and, when necessary, raising questions to stimulate discussion or bring the discussion back on track. The presenter should be careful not to stay too long at any group so that the members will not direct their questions to him or her.

At the 1- or 2-minute mark, the presenter should sound a warning that time is almost up. When the time has ended, the teacher or discussion leader reconvenes the group into the large group and calls for the reports of the buzz group recorders. After each group has reported, the presenter may want to open the floor to general discussion.

Depending on the complexity of the problem and the purpose of the discussion, the group recorders may be asked to get together later to summarize their findings into a report on the topic discussed.

Buzz groups with more than three people usually involve moving some chairs around so that each group can form its own circle. Circular seating enhances the discussion of each group and helps the members of the group become better acquainted with each other.

Variations of the Buzz Group

Phillips 66 Method

The Phillips 66 variation of buzz groups was developed by J. Donald Phillips. It can be used with small groups or large groups. With this system, the large group is divided into small groups of six persons with as little movement of chairs as possible. The subgroups are then given a 6-minute time limit to discuss the issue or problem.

Clark's 22 Method

The Clark's 22 method is best used when there is little possibility for movement in the room, such as in a large auditorium with stationary seats. Two people discuss the topic for 2 minutes. The presenter or discussion leader then calls for reports from each group.

Huddle Method

In the huddle method, 5 or 6 people meet to discuss the problem. It is much like a football or basketball game huddle wherein the group quickly discusses the alternatives and devises a plan. In the huddle method, the group usually begins by choosing a "captain" or "quarterback" to lead the discussion. Holmes and Mortensen (1983) state that huddle groups are productive because the small group is conducive to natural, nonforced, informal conversation.

Circular Response Method

This method is very similar to the general buzz group method except that responses to the problem or issue are presented according to seating arrangement in the circle. It ensures participation of each group member.

Progressive Buzz Sessions

The progressive sessions are very similar to the general buzz group method except that at a specified time, the groups rotate both topic questions and contributions. This allows each group to work on a number of different topics and still benefit from the written contributions of other group members.

Appropriate Uses, Suggestions, and Cautions

The buzz group method is best used to enhance discussion, especially when the overall group is large. It helps identify the needs and interests of a learning group and sets up a situation where the strong help the weak in a team effort.

Another appropriate use of the buzz group is to get the members acquainted with each other. Often, short versions of the buzz group, such as the Clark's 22 method or Phillips 66 method, can be used as icebreakers or get-acquainted methods.

Buzz groups can also be used when the presenter becomes aware that there are several class members who are hesitant to speak up before the large group. Often the buzz group method helps draw those people out and obtain their contributions.

Buzz groups also allow a large audience to help evaluate the learning experience. Sometimes suggestions for improving a meeting can be developed in a buzz group setting.

Advantages, Disadvantages, and Limitations of the Buzz Group

When using the buzz group instructional strategy, the presenter should be aware of the following advantages, disadvantages, and limitations of this technique.

Advantages of the Buzz Group

1. It allows everyone's ideas to be expressed.
2. Participants learn to work in real-life situations where others' opinions are considered.
3. It sets the groundwork to get discussion started.
4. Because members are expressing opinions, it is good for dealing with controversial subjects.

Disadvantages of the Buzz Group

1. Effectiveness of the group may be lowered by the immature behavior of a few.
2. It may not be effective for younger groups or groups that know each other too well to take each other's opinions seriously.
3. It can be time-consuming when dealing with very large groups.

Limitations of the Buzz Group

1. The group must be well prepared by the teacher in order to keep the group on topic.
2. It is not intended to be a full meeting but used as a supplement to other methods.

Examples or Applications

Buzz groups are most frequently used in combination with the lecture method, which enhances both techniques. Buzz groups can be used to solve a problem, decide on a question to ask the presenter, or review information that has been previously reported.

Once the buzz group reports are given, the teacher has several options. Each recorder and leader can be asked to prepare a short written report on what was discussed, including any revisions made during the group discussion. The recorders can all get together and prepare a full report. Or, during the discussion that follows the buzz group reports, the teacher can outline a plan of action based on the findings of the groups. If necessary, the buzz groups can stay together and become study committees.

Summary

The buzz group is an excellent means of getting total participation by large groups. With a well-prepared presenter and good discussion, the buzz group can be a lively and effective means of learning. Ryan (1992) points out that buzz groups are ideal for the exploration of topics and the revelation of individual and collective opinion.

References

Bellon, J., Bellon, E., & Blank, M. (1992). *Teaching from a research knowledge base.* New York: Merrill.

Holmes, D., & Mortensen, M. (1983). *Discussion techniques for adult educators.* Utah State University, Conference and Institute Division. (ERIC Document Reproduction Service No. ED 245 065)

The Professional Teacher Education Module Series. (1984). *Employ brainstorming, buzz group, and question box techniques* (2nd ed., Module C-3 of Category C—Instructional Execution). Columbus: Ohio State University, National Center for Research in Vocational Education. (ERIC Document Reproduction Service No. 244 136)

Ryan, C. (1992). *Case studies in teacher education: A series for working with students at risk.* Wilberforce, OH: Central State University. (ERIC Document Reproduction Service No. ED 358 063)

Williams, D. (1983). *Using the discussion group technique in the ESL conversation class.* (ERIC Document Reproduction Service No. ED 230 022)

The Buzz Group Planning Sheet

Date:_____Time:_____Site:_____

Overall Purpose(s) of Session:

Objective(s) of Buzz Session:

Issue(s)/Question(s) for Group Discussion:

    1.

    2.

    3.

Group Formation:

    Group Size:

    Directions for Forming:

Directions for Group Participation (including discussion and sharing phases):

Set-up Needs:

Handouts:

Summary Notes:

The Buzz Group Evaluation Sheet

(You may wish to have someone else consider these items,
as well as evaluating yourself.)

Was the purpose of the group appropriate for the overall
purpose of the learning session? __Yes __No (Explain)

Were directions for forming the group followed?
__Yes __No (Explain)

Was the issue/question for discussion clearly explained?
__Yes __No (Explain)

How well did each group remain on task during the discussion
time?

How well did each group share its thoughts with the entire
group?

How adequate was the time allocation for
. . . group discussion?
. . . group sharing?

How well did the classroom practitioner bring summary/
conclusion to the overall session?

Were set-up arrangements satisfactory?
__Yes __No (Explain)

If handouts were needed, were they
. . . available?
. . . satisfactory?

What was the best aspect of the overall session?

Suggestions for improvement:

9

Programmed Instruction

Definition

Programmed instruction is a self-learning type of instruction that uses a workbook, textbook, or electronic device (such as a computer) to instruct participants and help them attain a specific level of performance.

Introduction

Programmed instruction is a self-paced form of instruction. It provides small steps that guide the participants through the material with questions, answers, situations, and even tests. The material is presented in a controlled sequence of steps.

The learner participates by responding, checking the answer, and then proceeding to the next step. The materials are designed for individual use, but could in some instances be used in group situations.

Typically, programmed instruction is thought of as computer-assisted instruction (CAI) or computer-managed instruction (CMI), but automated or computer teaching is only one type of programmed instruction. The method can also use written material, workbooks, or films.

Main Procedural Steps in Using Programmed Instruction

Selecting materials for the programmed instruction method is the most important hurdle to choosing an effective program. Materials can be bought, teacher made, student made, or borrowed. If separate answer sheets are used, the materials can be reused, especially when they cover basic concepts.

The leader or presenter must be familiar with the materials and be prepared to guide the participant in the proper use of the material.

Once the materials are selected, attention should be given to the physical setting. The setting should be free of distractions and offer the students room to work.

Explaining how to use the materials is the next step. The proper use of the answer sheets, the workbooks, or the computer should be carefully covered and demonstrated.

Learning from programmed instruction is different from other learning techniques, and participants need to be prepared for this. The main difference is that it is an individualized method and does not involve group interaction.

If programmed textbooks or workbooks are being used, the participants should be cautioned that looking ahead for the answers will result in less learning for them and they will be penalizing themselves. Because each learner proceeds at his or her own pace, the participants should be encouraged to feel confident without looking ahead at the answers.

As the participants begin, the presenter should quietly supervise each participant to make sure that he or she is using the materials correctly.

Programmed instruction involves active and continuous participation by the participants and may be more tiring and demanding than other classroom teaching methods. It is best to keep the programmed learning portion of the class time relatively brief. The method is very adaptable and can easily be supplemented with other materials and methods.

Toward the end of the class time, the lesson or unit should be summarized by the participants. This provides a good opportunity to check how well the students understood and retained the information contained in the program. Gibbons (1993) believes that feedback presents the participant with reinforcement that in turn helps build critical-thinking skills for making future decisions.

Variations of Programmed Instruction

Programmed instruction is a very broad term that is filled with variations. First, and most simply, the medium through which the material is presented can be either books and workbooks, films, textbooks, or computers. In addition, the programmed material can be one of four types: linear, branching, combination, and mathetics.

Linear Programs

The linear program is identical for all students and is done in sequence units. Each participant responds, checks the answer, and then proceeds to the next frame. The same procedure is followed throughout the program.

Branching Programs

Branching is done with a series of frames or units. The sequence that the participant follows is determined by his or her response to the previous question. If the answer was correct, the participant may be directed to skip some information, provided information concerning the next topic, or given more in-depth information on the original topic. A wrong answer may lead the participant to information concerning why the wrong answer was chosen or require him or her to return to the base frame and choose another response.

Combination Programs

Combination programs have the characteristics of both the linear and branching. Part of the program is linear and identical for all participants; another part is branching and depends on the participant's response.

Mathetics Programs

The mathetics program resembles the branching program but does not necessarily depend on the participant's response. Exercises are included that may be skipped entirely by participants already proficient in the subject but may be completed by participants needing more information.

Appropriate Uses, Suggestions, and Cautions

The use of programmed instruction is usually to provide individual instruction in a setting where participants can work at their own pace. It permits a large degree of self-teaching and can free the teacher for tasks that are less rote.

Programmed instruction can also be used successfully in teaching technical knowledge or knowledge related to occupations.

The technique can be used to provide basic or remedial instruction or help participants catch up on material that was missed due to absences.

Simsek (1993) argues that programmed instruction restricts the learner to an isolated, controlled environment that limits other learning experiences and peer socialization. Tudor and Bostow (1991) feel that programmed instruction is used incorrectly in the classroom because current software masks the basic operant learning principles that B. F. Skinner praised so highly.

Caution is needed to make sure that the programmed instruction materials used are suited to the course or the learners' needs. The method should not be used over long periods of time or very often as students tend to get tired and bored with too much of this type of instruction.

Advantages, Disadvantages, and Limitations of Programmed Instruction

When using the programmed instruction instructional strategy, the presenter should be aware of the following advantages, disadvantages and limitations of this technique.

Advantages of Programmed Instruction

1. It is self-paced so that each participant can move through at his or her own speed.
2. The presenter is freed from having to present routine information.

3. The format is organized and sequenced for individual readiness.
4. Participants can learn independently in either a formal or an informal setting.
5. A single presenter can monitor a large lab of participants.
6. There is a low error rate in the material presented.
7. There is a high quality of learning for all students because of the individual pacing.
8. Feedback is immediate.
9. Participants actively participate in the learning process.
10. Participants can study programs that are not part of the ordinary curriculum.

Disadvantages of Programmed Instruction

1. Materials must be properly prepared and tested.
2. Some participants become bored with materials.
3. Participants may finish at different times, which can cause problems with scheduling and subsequent training.
4. Quality materials that fit existing curricula are limited.
5. It is not applicable to psychomotor learning.
6. Some participants find the programs repetitious.

Limitations of Programmed Instruction

1. Good programs are hard to identify and not all programs are worth using.
2. Programs are difficult to write and require considerable planning, testing, and revising to make sure no steps are left out of the sequence.
3. The cost of the materials, machines, and computers can be prohibitive.

Examples or Applications

Programmed instruction can be used for standard subjects such as science, math, and history, as well as for occupational educational subjects. Computer-aided instruction (CAI) now has programs that cover a wide range of subjects. Ellson (1986) states that the programmed learning method is beneficial because it provides the learner with constructive feedback on the accuracy of the participant's answer.

In addition, CAI can take many forms, including instructional games, modeling, simulation, tutorial, inquiry, and drill and practice.

Summary

Programmed instruction allows presenters to spend less time teaching rote learning and memorization. Programmed materials can be used by all levels of students, including gifted and slow learners. Programmed instruction can result in increased individual achievement. Hannafin and Savenye (1993) state that many presenters praise computer-assisted learning programs because they allow participants to be interactive in a self-paced way, not just passive recipients of lecture-based information, and allow the presenter to take on the role of facilitator.

References

Ellson, D. (1986). Improving productivity in teaching. *Phi Delta Kappan, 68*(2), 111-124.

Gibbons, A. (1993). Interactive instruction and feedback. *Educational Technology and Development, 41*(4), 104-108.

Hannafin, R., & Savenye, S. (1993). Technology in the classroom: The teacher's new role and resistance to it. *Educational Technology, 33*(6), 26-31.

Simsek, A. (1993). *The effects of learner control and group composition in computer-based cooperative learning.* New Orleans, LA: Proceedings of Selected Research and Development Presentations at the Convention of the Association for Educational Communications and Technology, Sponsored by the Research and Theory Division. (ERIC Document Reproduction Service No. ED 362 205)

Tudor, R., & Bostow, D. (1991). Computer-programmed instruction: The relation of required interaction of practical application. *Journal of Applied Behavior Analysis, 24*(2), 361-368.

The Programmed Instruction
Planning Sheet

Date:_____Time:_____Site:_____

Learning Objective(s):

Procedure(s):

Materials Needed:

Additional Activities for Those Who Finish Early:

Plan for Checking for Understanding:

Follow-up Activity(ies):

Summary Notes:

The Programmed Instruction
Evaluation Sheet

(🍎You may wish to have someone else consider these items,
as well as evaluating yourself.)

Were the materials appropriate for participants' needs?
   __Yes __No (Explain)

Were site provisions adequate? __Yes __No (Explain)

🍎What was the level of enthusiasm of the classroom
   practitioner?

🍎What was the level of enthusiasm of the classroom
   participants?

🍎How effective was the check for understanding?

🍎What was the best aspect of this learning session?

🍎Was follow-up activity used?
      __Yes (If so, were directions clear?) __No (Explain)

🍎Suggestions for improvement:

10
Directed Study

Definition

Reading selected theory and factual material in a controlled situation and under the direction and guidance of a leader or teacher is called a directed study.

Introduction

Directed study is a means of presenting information to a group and then immediately checking to see if the facts and knowledge contained in that information have been learned. It steps beyond the bounds of making reading assignments for homework or work outside the classroom because the reading is done in the presence of a presenter and questions are asked following each reading.

Gee and Rakow (1990) surveyed 100 social studies teachers and found that the teachers preferred teacher-directed instruction because it proved more helpful for the participants in many areas including "notetaking, using a reading and study method such as survey/question/read/recite/review (SQ3R), outlining and concept mapping, and summary writing" (p. 400).

Main Procedural Steps in Using Directed Study

Selecting appropriate reading material is the first step in a successful directed study teaching situation. The presenter or group leader must be careful to ensure that textbooks, reference books, or articles contain the material that is pertinent to the subject at hand. The material must also be at a level of comprehension suitable for the group and short enough to be included in a directed study situation.

The reading material should be broken into short sections, with each segment covering a complete idea. Only a few well-chosen new items of information should be presented in each session.

Once the material has been selected and a suitable atmosphere for learning has been found, the directed study session begins with each participant being given the reading material. Instruct the group to read the first section and close their books or cover the pages when completed.

When all have finished, the presenter then asks questions based on the information that has just been read. The questions should concentrate on the factual information and not on problem solving or application. At this stage of the directed study, it is the factual information that is important.

Points of confusion may require the teacher to read selected segments aloud or direct the class to reread the information. Sometimes the presenter may need to offer illustrations to supplement the reading in order to enhance understanding.

The steps are then repeated for each segment that has been chosen. After all segments have been read, a general question-and-answer period will help to pull all the information together. At the end of the question-and-answer period, the teacher should summarize, going over the key facts that have been read in this session.

Directed study must be kept to no more than 40 minutes. It requires an intense level of concentration on the part of the readers that cannot be sustained over a long period of time.

Following the presentation of information, the application portion of the lesson begins. This part of the lesson requires the readers to use the information they have just learned, either in hands-on practices or to make decisions, problem solve, or form judgments.

Directed study is concerned with the presentation and retention of facts. Once the student has a grasp of the facts, he or she will be able to reflect on the knowledge, analyze it, and try to solve the problem.

Variations of Directed Study

The main variation of this technique is outside reading assignments. Directed study and outside reading can be used with large or small groups. Because it is presenter-directed study, it is suitable for almost all participants and can even be used for individuals. Although the mere reading of material does not assure retention or comprehension, directed study removes the variable found in outside study—bad study habits.

Directed study will enhance study habits outside the classroom and may eventually lead to participants' developing good study habits and the tools to be motivated for self-study.

Appropriate Uses, Suggestions, and Cautions

Directed study is inappropriate for teaching skills, but it is an effective means of presenting factual information to large or small groups.

Caution should be taken in selecting the material. Too many new segments of facts will hinder the retention process. On the other hand, if carefully managed and followed with good questions that stress the facts, the directed study method can have a high retention rate. The presenter is able to check his or her progress immediately during the questioning period. In addition, the presenter has the opportunity to clear up any misinformation or lack of understanding of the facts. Wakefield (1993) cautions that within directed instruction, if the presenter chooses to *rigidly direct* instead of *guide*, then he or she removes the opportunity for the participants to develop independence and confidence in original thought.

Neilsen (1990) cautions that the teacher-directed study is too objective and does not allow for improvisation on the part of the presenter and participant. He concludes that it does not promote the emergence of affective qualities found in alternative learning practices.

Advantages, Disadvantages, and Limitations of Directed Study

When using the directed study instructional strategy, the presenter should be aware of the following advantages, disadvantages, and limitations of this technique.

Advantages of Directed Study

1. The controlled conditions with the presenter present during the learning are effective for almost all students.
2. The presenter does not have to depend on a single textbook to cover the course under study.

3. It works equally well with large or small groups.
4. There is high retention of factual information.
5. It can lead to the development of good individual study habits.
6. There is immediate feedback from participant to presenter or teacher.

Disadvantages of Directed Study

1. It demands close attention and concentration from both participant and presenter or teacher.
2. Only a few factual items can be covered at each sitting.
3. Slow readers may slow down the process and leave faster readers with long waits between reading segments.
4. It delays discussion of questions that deal with reflective thinking and problem solving.

Limitations of Directed Study

1. Facts may have little meaning to participants until they are applied in real-life situations.
2. It cannot be sustained over a long period of time.
3. It is not suitable for learning skills or for hands-on type of study.
4. The atmosphere must be conducive to studying; participants must be quiet and able to be supervised by the presenter or teacher.
5. Paul (1988) says that teacher-directed learning does not allow the participant the freedom to play an active role in his or her own learning process.

Examples or Applications

Outside study or readings have not proven to be very effective ways of relating factual information, largely due to participants' not having good study habits. With directed study, the material can be presented and the reader questioned for understanding right in the classroom. It is best used before other, more interactive techniques such as discussion or problem solving.

By combining directed study with other, more active and lively techniques, the presenter can be assured that the participants have a base of information before they begin reflective thinking and problem solving. Although it is not suitable for presenting skills, such as shop subjects, it is excellent for presenting shop theory, instructions, and descriptive material. The directed study can then be followed up with techniques that are effective for learning skills.

Summary

Directed study will probably never be a day-to-day classroom teaching method. It does have some very practical applications and is useful in presenting, and then checking, factual information. Once learned, that factual information can provide a strong base for moving to other learning techniques. In addition, Brent and DiObilda (1993) praise direct instruction because it provides the presenter with structured learning practices and a presenter's guide that encourages positive reinforcement and immediate feedback based on participants' correct and incorrect choices.

References

Brent, G., & DiObilda, N. (1993). Effects of curriculum alignment versus direct instruction on urban children. *Journal of Educational Research, 86*(6), 333-338.

Gee, T., & Rakow, S. (1990). Helping students learn by reading: What experienced social studies teachers have learned. *Social Education, 54*(6), 398-401.

Neilsen, L. (1990). To be a good teacher: Growing beyond the garden path. *Reading Teacher, 44*(2), 152-153.

Paul, R. (1988). *Two conflicting theories of knowledge, learning, and literacy: The didactic and the critical* (Resource Publication, Series 1, No. 2). Upper Montclair, NJ: Montclair State College, Institute for Critical Thinking (ERIC Document Reproduction Service No. ED 352 327)

Wakefield, A. (1993). Developmentally appropriate practice: Figuring things out. *Educational Forum, 57*(2), 134-143.

The Directed Study Planning Sheet

Date:_____Time:_____Site:_____

Criteria for Materials Selection:

Materials to Be Used:

Sections to Be Studied:

Learning Objectives:

Vocabulary:

Procedure:

Questions to Check Level of Understanding:

Application (activity, directions):

Criteria for Satisfactory Completion of Application Phase:

Supplemental Activity for Those Who Complete Assignment Early:

Summary Notes:

The Directed Study
Evaluation Sheet

(🍎You may wish to have someone else consider these items,
as well as evaluating yourself.)

🍎Did participants appear to understand the learning objectives
for this session? __Yes __No (Explain)

🍎Were concepts presented clearly? __Yes __No (Explain)

🍎Were necessary vocabulary words and phrases defined?
__Yes __No (Explain)

🍎How enthusiastic was the classroom practitioner?

What was the level of enthusiasm among participants?

Were all necessary materials and equipment needed available?
__Yes __No (Explain)

How adequate were the basic instructional materials for the
learning objectives?

🍎How adequate was the check for understanding?

🍎Were directions clear? __Yes __No (Explain)

🍎How effective was the summary for clarification?

🍎How effective was the summary for closure?

🍎What was best about this session?

🍎Suggestions for improvement:

11

Experiment

Definition

The experiment is a way of teaching based on research and investigation. In the experiment method, the learner studies a basic principle by applying that principle and then observing the results.

Introduction

The experiment is used to clarify information that the learner already knows or to try to discover unknown information. In the classroom, the experiment is most effectively used to verify a basic principle by conducting an experiment that will prove or disprove the principle by observing the results. Experiments for pure research are seldom effective in the classroom.

The experiment is a way to collect information, classify that information on the basis of the activity, evaluate the information, and then draw conclusions based on what has been seen. Retention rate is high for the experiment method as long as the experiment works.

The experiment is best used in the teaching of scientific principles but need not be limited to that area.

Main Procedural Steps
in Using the Experiment

For an experiment to be an effective teaching tool, the experiment must work. Trying to explain why an experiment fails defeats the purpose of the exercise and confuses the learner.

To help ensure success, the leader or teacher should follow these six steps:

1. Make sure the participants understand the principle under consideration.
2. Outline in detail the steps to be taken in the experiment.
3. If the participants are going to develop their own plan for testing the principle, the leader or teacher should carefully check the plan before they begin.
4. Require a report on the results of the experiment. This enables the teacher to see if the student observed and confirmed the principle or just "rigged" the experiment to give the expected result.
5. Check and recheck all equipment and materials. Carefully prepare any materials necessary to use in the experiment.
6. Keep the experiment within the realm of understanding and skill of the learners. Do not offer experiments that will not give conclusive results in the eyes of the learners.

In preparing a way to study the results of the experiment, the leader or teacher may need to help the participants set up their charts, graphs, or whatever means they are using to measure results. Check to be sure that these are set up so that insignificant and irrelevant data can be eliminated.

Experiments can be done in a group, in pairs, in subgroups, or individually. If materials are limited, the leader or teacher can perform the experiment for the whole group while each records his or her own observations.

Variations of the Experiment

Experiments can be used to verify and impress on participants existing laws and principles. This is done not to teach the participants the principle but for the sake of emphasis, retention, and complete understanding.

Experiments can also be used to improve practices or processes by searching for better ways to carry out the procedure. Henson (1993) offers simulation as an experimental way of learning that allows participants to put themselves in hypothetical situations in order to problem solve.

Another type of experiment is research. In research, the participants are attempting to find a solution to a problem or theory for which no satisfactory answer has yet been found. The research method typically requires mature and trained participants.

Sometimes leaders or teachers will attempt to combine the research and verification methods by withholding the knowledge of the principle until after the experiment has been completed. Although the thrill of discovery may be stronger in those situations, so is the percentage of failure. Few students have the degree of imagination and discipline to observe the outcome of the experiment and arrive at the basic principle.

Appropriate Uses, Suggestions, and Cautions

Experiments are most often used to verify scientific knowledge. It is not a method that is suitable for presenting skills or discovering scientific laws.

Caution should be used in choosing experiments. A failed experiment is a failed lesson. The experimental techniques should be well within the ability of the group and provide results that are conclusive. The principles should be presented before the experiment by other methods, such as lecture.

As a teaching method, the experiment should be used to verify, not to discover. Roth (1994) believes that learning through the use of experiments yields experience with "situated learning, total learning environments, self-directed project activity, authentic practice and collaborative learning" (p. 219), which are all current practices in education instruction that extend into the workplace.

Advantages, Disadvantages, and Limitations of the Experiment

When using the experiment instructional strategy, the leader or teacher should be aware of the following advantages, disadvantages, and limitations of this technique.

Advantages of the Experiment

1. It is excellent for verifying technical information.
2. Hands-on experiments increase retention rate.
3. It calls for analysis and careful observation.
4. It is a good technique to mix with other, less interactive techniques, such as the lecture.

Disadvantages of the Experiment

1. It is limited in subject use; most effective in teaching related science.
2. It is not suitable for teaching skills.
3. It requires a base of knowledge of the principle to be studied before experiment begins.
4. Unless carefully chosen and prepared, it can have a high degree of failure, which negates the purpose of the experiment.

Limitations of the Experiment

1. The research type of experimentation is best for mature, trained participants.
2. Required materials and suitable equipment can be costly.
3. Osborne and Freyberg (1985) state that often experiments are merely controlled demonstrations in which the participant and teacher already know the desired result, leaving no room for experimentation in the truest sense.

Examples or Applications

Many scientific laws can be verified in the classroom with simple experiments. In addition, in teaching shop or other vocational classes, many of the practices used are based on scientific principles, and experiments can be used to verify and emphasize those practices.

Summary

The experiment method is most often used for science, chemistry, physics, or to test principles that skills are based on. In the experiment method, information and principles are presented by other means, then verified by the experiment. Based on their observations of the experiment, participants collect the information, classify it, evaluate it, and then make deductions.

References

Henson, K. T. (1993). *Methods and strategies for teaching in secondary and middle schools*. New York: Longman.

Osborne, R., & Freyberg, P. (1985). *Learning in science*. Hong Kong: Heinemann.

Roth, W. M. (1994). Experimenting in a constructivist high school physics laboratory. *Journal of Research in Science Teaching, 31*(2), 197-223.

The Experiment Planning Sheet

Date:_____Time:_____Site:_____

Title of Experiment:

Purpose of Experiment:

Concept(s):

Vocabulary:

Procedures and Directions:

Handouts:

Equipment Needed:

Materials Needed:

Summary Notes:

The Experiment Evaluation Sheet

(🍎You may wish to have someone else consider these items,
as well as evaluating yourself.)

Was the experiment appropriate for teaching the stated concept?
__Yes __No (Explain)

Was the experiment designed to be a true investigation?
__Yes __No (Explain)

🍎Were vocabulary words defined well? __Yes __No (Explain)

Did participants appear to have necessary prerequisites for this
lesson? __Yes __No (Explain)

🍎Was the procedure adequately explained before students began
working? __Yes __No (Explain)

🍎Were the handouts helpful? __Yes __No (Explain)

Was there a check for understanding regarding
    . . . basic principles?
    . . . vocabulary?
    . . . procedure and directions?
    __Yes __No (Explain)
🍎How effectively were participants' questions handled?

Were most participants successful in performing the experiment?
    __Yes __No (Explain)
Was there a check for understanding at the end of the session?
    __Yes __No (Explain)
🍎Did the classroom practitioner summarize the lesson effectively?
    __Yes __No (Explain)

Was the time allocated adequately? __Yes __No (Explain)

What provisions were made for participants who might finish early?

🍎How enthusiastic was the classroom practitioner?

How much enthusiasm was there among participants?

🍎What aspects of the lesson were most effective?

🍎Suggestions for improvement:

12

Brainstorming

Definition

Brainstorming is a technique that solicits creative ideas through imagination instead of judicial reasoning. It stimulates creativity and cooperation.

Introduction

Brainstorming is a free-wheeling session used to solicit ideas or look for solutions to problems. It is a good change of pace for most classrooms. In the first part of brainstorming, the group is concerned only with quantity. Only after the brainstorming session is over does the group direct its attention to objective judgment of the ideas presented.

Hirokawa (1990) suggests that the pooling in a collective manner of information by individuals in a group helps determine the difference between viable and impossible decisions and ultimately leads to effective communication and decision making.

Main Procedural Steps in Using Brainstorming

Brainstorming sessions must first begin with a specific topic or problem. The topic is usually best phrased as a question and should be narrow enough in scope to encourage specific ideas and not broad generalizations.

The teacher or leader should carefully explain how to brainstorm and set the ground rules for the brainstorming session as follows:

1. Offer suggestions one at a time.
2. All ideas expressed are welcomed as long as they pertain to the topic or problem under discussion.
3. Evaluation and criticism are not allowed.
4. Judgment of ideas is postponed until a later time.
5. "Hitchhiking" on other people's ideas is encouraged, especially if they offer a new slant on the original idea and add creativity.
6. "It won't work" statements are not allowed.
7. Quantity is wanted. The more ideas offered, no matter how wild, the better.

The teacher or leader may act as the facilitator for the groups or each group may select its own. The facilitator or chairperson should keep a passive attitude and not let his or her opinion be known. He or she is responsible for keeping the group on the subject, stopping any criticism of ideas, and seeing that the rules are enforced.

In addition, each group needs a recorder to write down the ideas presented. If individual brainstorming is used, each person can write down his or her own ideas.

Allow 30 seconds to a minute after the situation or problem has been presented for participants to collect their thoughts. Then begin the brainstorming session, which usually should last no more than 30 minutes. At the 1-minute mark, the chairperson or teacher should sound a warning.

At the end of the allowed time, each recorder should read aloud or write on the board all the suggestions of the group. The list can then be screened, either by the brainstorming group or collectively by the whole group.

Suggestions may be screened by dividing them into four or more groups:

1. Ideas most likely to succeed
2. Best ideas for short range
3. Best ideas for long range
4. Ideas that can be pretested before adoption

In dealing with wild or off-the-wall ideas, either reject them immediately or look for parts of the idea that may be sound.

Remind the participants after the brainstorming session that their brains will probably keep storming for several days, and they should continue to write down any further ideas they think of to share at a later date.

The seating arrangement in brainstorming needs to be close enough for people to see each other and respond to ideas.

Variations of Brainstorming

Variations of the brainstorming technique are simply a matter of how large the group is. A whole class or large group can engage in brainstorming with the teacher acting as recorder and chairperson. This is the simplest form of brainstorming.

Brainstorming can also be done by breaking the overall group into smaller groups of 12 to 15 people. The most effective brainstorming is done in groups of this size. In addition, it ensures that everyone will have a chance to offer ideas.

Solo brainstorming is done on an individual basis and does not afford the same kind of atmosphere as group brainstorming. Participants are usually reluctant to write down their own wild ideas unless they hear others offering ideas off the top of their heads.

Appropriate Uses, Suggestions, and Cautions

Brainstorming is effective when used in problem-solving situations. It is also appropriate for vocational courses and for any topic that demands creative thinking. The topics could be, for example, deciding on names for a new product, figuring out incentives to get more students to join in an art project, or finding ways to protect children from diseases.

Caution should be taken to keep a few vocal participants from dominating the group and intimidating other members. It is also possible that some students will not take the task seriously. In brainstorming ideas, it is important to make sure that participants don't confuse spontaneity with silliness. Russell and Lane (1993) believe that too much reliance on brainstorming will prevent the participants from seeing an idea in front of them because the participants feel that the idea appears when one is not searching frantically for it.

Advantages, Disadvantages, and Limitations of Brainstorming

When using the brainstorming instructional strategy, the teacher should be aware of the following advantages, disadvantages, and limitations of this technique.

Advantages of Brainstorming

1. Encourages cooperative thinking
2. Promotes creative thinking
3. Adds variety and zest to the classroom
4. Can lead participants to change their attitudes toward the ideas of others
5. Creates a nonthreatening atmosphere that can encourage students who do not usually participate to join in
6. Is relatively economical in terms of time
7. Does not require elaborate classroom arrangement
8. Eliminates arguments during discussion

Disadvantages of Brainstorming

1. It can be monopolized by overenthusiastic members.
2. Recording all comments and ideas during the session could slow the spontaneous flow of ideas.
3. Its ultimate value may come from participation rather than from any of the ideas generated.
4. It needs a good group leader to keep negative comments down and ensure that it does not get out of hand.
5. Students may not take the brainstorming session seriously.
6. Davis (1992) argues that forced group thinking may replace creative individual thought.

Limitations of Brainstorming

1. It works best with small groups of 12 to 15 people.
2. It is most effective if the process is explained ahead of time.
3. Uneasiness on the part of participants can bog down the session.
4. Normally only 10% of the group's ideas are ultimately usable.

Examples or Applications

In choosing questions for brainstorming, questions that begin with "In what ways . . ." "What are some other uses for . . ." or "List as many improvements as you can for . . ." are usually good places to start. The technique has been used extensively in business and industry settings. Burton (1990) reports that (a) 65% to 93% more ideas are generated within a group than by individual decision making,

(b) competition heightens creative thinking by 50%, and (c) groups that brainstorm make better decisions than regular discussion groups. It can be used in the classroom to attack problems in the same way.

Any project that involves creative thinking lends itself to a brainstorming technique. In addition, teachers or leaders can use brainstorming to get the group to address problems that may be present in the classroom or to deal with the gripes of some of the participants.

Summary

From the offices on Madison Avenue to the teaching profession comes the brainstorming technique. Brainstorming can open up the classroom or training session with a free-wheeling, fast-moving session that is designed both to solicit new ideas and open up the doors to creativity. Mongeau (1993) states that Alex Osborn founded brainstorming on the premise of competitive camaraderie among group members that encourages idea generation and motivation to create. Its use encourages participation and openness and can foster a more tolerant atmosphere.

References

Burton, G. E. (1990). The measurements of distortion tendencies induced by the win-lose nature of in-group loyalty. *Small Group Research, 21*(1), 128-141.

Davis, G. (1992). *Creativity is forever.* Dubuque, IA: Kendall/Hunt.

Hirokawa, R. Y. (1990). The role of communication in group decision-making efficacy. *Small Group Research, 21*(2), 190-204.

Mongeau, P. A. (1993, February 12-16). *The brainstorming myth.* Paper presented at the 64th annual meeting of the Western States Communication Association, Albuquerque, NM.

Russell, J., & Lane, R. (1993). *Kleppner's adverstising procedure.* Englewood Cliffs, NJ: Prentice Hall.

The Brainstorming Planning Sheet

Date:_____Time:_____Site:_____

Purpose of Overall Session:

Purpose of Brainstorming Segment:

Question(s) to Be Considered:

Directions for Group Formation (if there will be more than one group):

Directions for Small-Group Participation:

Directions for Sharing Ideas Within the Large Group:

Time Allocated for Brainstorming:

Time Allocated for Sharing of Ideas:

Materials Needed:

Handouts:

Summary Notes:

The Brainstorming Evaluation Sheet

(You may wish to have someone else consider these items,
as well as evaluating yourself.)

Was the brainstorming question appropriate for the topic?
__Yes __No (Explain)

Was the brainstorming question appropriate for these participants? __Yes __No (Explain)

Were directions clear? __Yes __No (Explain)

Were time allocations suitable?

What was the level of interest among participants?

Was the facilitator enthusiastic? __Yes __No (Explain)

How useful were the ideas generated?

Did anyone tend to monopolize the group? If so, how did the facilitator handle the situation?

Were necessary materials readily avilable?

Was the summary effective in bringing closure?
__Yes __No (Explain)

What was especially effective about this session?

Suggestions for improvement:

13

Questioning

Definition

Questioning is a method used by a presenter to elicit a verbal response from a participant, allowing the presenter to determine what the participant has learned. It is a way to discover and interpret information. Effective questioning encourages the participant to think critically and provides feedback to the presenter about participant understanding.

Introduction

Oral questioning can be very effective in promoting participant learning. Participant motivation and participation can be activated by effective questioning. It also provides for active involvement on behalf of the participant. Participants are given practice in revealing their ideas to the presenter and their peers. Ideas shared among participants add variety and knowledge to the class. Oral questions may be directed at one person, a small group, or a large group. The questioning method provides excellent training for communicating well in a future job.

If questions are asked in a logical order by the presenter, they can help the participant to think logically. It is important to help participants learn to think in different ways. Participants will stay alert and interested when questions require them to do more than just remember.

Main Procedural Steps in Using Questioning

When using the questioning method, the presenter must decide which type of strategy to use. But all should have certain objectives in common. Questioning proves most effective when used to:

✓ Introduce, summarize, or review a competency
✓ Clarify previous points
✓ Promote understanding
✓ Help participants use ideas rather than remember them
✓ Provide presenters with feedback on how much participants are learning

Two types of questions are most frequently used by participants—narrow and broad.

Narrow Questions

Narrow questions require little imaginative or deep thinking; they ask for factual information and responses that are predictable. The answers are specific, so the participant either knows them or does not know them.

Presenters generally use this method of questioning when drilling or testing reading comprehension. Narrow questions are a way of going over facts and reviewing for basic understanding. This method should be used to make a transition from lower levels of thinking to higher cognitive levels.

Broad Questions

Broad questions command a plethora of different possible responses. Thus, responses to this type of questioning are not predictable. The questions are purposefully thoughtful to promote critical thinking on behalf of the participant. The participant will most likely respond with answers that convey judgment, feelings, or opinions.

Broad questions are used to make participants experiment with their options and analyze consequences. These are especially helpful with problem-solving situations. Independent thinking and creativity are expressed as participants move away from basic recall to evaluative thinking.

Both of these questioning strategies are helpful when used at the appropriate time. But first, the presenter should know how to question his or her participants in a way that will be beneficial to both. The procedure for questioning involves five steps: planning questions, asking questions, handling partially correct and complete correct answers, handling incorrect answers, and handling no answer at all.

Step 1: Planning Questions

Presenters should carefully plan questions. Poor questions do not help participants learn. Presenters should know how to plan and use good questions. According to Cheek (1989), instructors should use questions to review or summarize lessons, assess what participants actually know prior to covering new content, promote understanding, and make participants think. He further suggests that instructors should attempt to emphasize important and factual information that is being taught and provide feedback during and after material is presented. The following should be kept in mind when planning questions:

- ✓ Make your questions short enough for the participants to remember.
- ✓ Include only one idea for each question.
- ✓ State the question using language familiar to the participant.
- ✓ Word questions so as to require participants to answer more than "Yes" or "No."
- ✓ Use questions that are related to the material being learned.
- ✓ State the question in such a way that the answer is not suggested.
- ✓ Avoid repeating questions in several different forms. Choose clear wording and remain consistent.
- ✓ Ask questions in a logical sequence.
- ✓ Design questions to measure understanding of the subject being learned. Trick questions should be avoided.

Step 2: Asking Questions

A presenter should begin with a planned set of questions related to a specific objective. The session should then be conducted in the following way. First, ask a question of the group. Next, wait to allow participants to think of their own answers. Finally, call on a participant by name and give that participant time to answer.

When asking oral questions, do the following:

✓ Direct questions to an individual within the entire group to initiate a single participant response as opposed to many talking at once.

✓ Ask different participants in a small group so that each one has a chance to participate.

✓ Reward correct answers with positive responses such as "That's right" or "Good," but never discourage a participant who gives an incorrect answer. This leads to embarrassment and withdrawal.

✓ Do not repeat answers given by participants or deliver lectures on ideas introduced by participants.

✓ Call on participants in random order to promote attention to the subject being discussed.

✓ Encourage participants to go beyond the first answer. Help them expand an idea and back it up with facts.

✓ Bring other participants into the discussion by asking them to react to the first participant's answer.

✓ Allow a wait time of 3 to 5 seconds after asking a question before requesting participant response. Buttery and Michalak (1978) agree that this wait time allows participants to think about their answers and helps them to participate more readily, eliminating the ineffectual rapid-fire method of questioning.

Step 3: Handling Partially Correct Answers and Complete Correct Answers

When a participant's answer is partially correct:

✓ Give credit for the correct part.
✓ Work with the participant to improve his or her answer.
✓ Ask another participant to offer the other correct part.

If a participant's answer is totally correct, reward the participant with praise such as "Very good" or "That's correct." Praise encourages participant participation and provides positive reinforcement.

Step 4: Handling Incorrect Answers

When incorrect answers are given, a presenter should try to remain noncritical in his or her response. Some suggestions are as follows:

✓ Commend the participant for his or her effort, but point out that the main idea was overlooked.

✓ Ask the participant other questions to direct his or her thinking back to the topic and help the participant come to the correct answer on his or her own.

✓ Tell the participant to think about the question and that you will return to him or her for another try.

Step 5: Handling No Answer at All

It is important for a presenter to remember to never make a participant feel dumb, because he or she will be less likely to participate in future question-and-answer sessions. All honest answers should be accepted and used to develop further meaning. If a participant cannot answer the question,

✓ Ask another participant.

✓ Try rewording the question in simpler language.

✓ Teach the material over again.

Variations of the Questioning Technique

Within the two main types of questions, narrow and broad, there are four subtypes. Within narrow questions there are cognitive-memory and convergent. Broad questions can be broken down into divergent and evaluative.

Cognitive-Memory

Cognitive-memory questions are narrow questions that require basic thinking. They are easily answered with facts, definitions, and memorized material. Often, a one-word answer is all that is needed. Houston (1983) argues that this method is individualistic, ignoring the needs of a group, and lacks direction on the part of the presenter and participant.

Convergent

Convergent questions are not as narrow as cognitive-memory questions because the participant must put a cluster of facts together to form a basic idea. They demand an explanation, usually about the relationship between two concepts. These questions generally begin with "how" and "why" to elicit the best response.

Divergent

Divergent questions are broad in nature and ask a participant to predict, hypothesize, or infer when responding. A high level of thinking must be used by the student to examine his or her choices and present many acceptable, feasible responses. This method leads to creative thinking and interest in the subject matter and is helpful in problem solving.

Evaluative

Evaluative questions are the highest level of broad questions. The cognitive levels of the cognitive-memory, convergent, and divergent question methods are meshed together to help organize knowledge in order for the participant to answer with a response that judges, justifies a choice, or defends a particular stance. Evidence must reinforce the selected choice. This method fosters independent, evaluative thinking. Arnold, Atwood, and Rogers (1973) concur that questions that go beyond rote memorization help students process information at higher cognitive levels, thus proving more advantageous for the participant. However, Sampson, Strykowski, Weinstein, and Walberg (1987) offer evidence that there is no conclusive empirical data that links high-level cognitive questioning with academic achievement.

Appropriate Uses, Suggestions, and Cautions

Questions are the best way to begin the process of communication, stimulate thinking, and gain information. Questions allow people to formulate solutions to problems using collective and individual thought. They provide insight into how individuals think and process information, what their personality and interests are, and how they might practically apply what has been learned. Questioning is most often used for

✓ Giving directions
✓ Managing an environment
✓ Initating instruction

✓ Creating learning situations
✓ Evaluating learning
✓ Stimulating thinking
✓ Developing attitudes and feelings
✓ Creating interest and motivation
✓ Introducing insight and new possibilities

There are four types of questioning strategies that presenters should be cautioned against. The *first* is questioning that yields "Yes" or "No" responses. These answers require little thought on the part of the participant. Unfortunately, it is an easy, quick strategy for the presenter. The participants can easily guess and they do not have to show supporting evidence for their answers. It is not a strategy that measures how much a participant has learned.

The *second* is asking ambiguous questions. These encourage guessing on the part of the participant because they are not clear to begin with. Participants cannot form meaningful responses to something they do not understand in the first place. These questions are irrelevant to the lesson and result in rambling.

The *third* is "spoon-feeding" questions. These give too much guidance and lead the student to the presenter's already-chosen "right" answer. The answer is so visible that it is worthless to even ask the question. This strategy encourages the participant to be lazy and sloppy in his or her thinking.

The *fourth* is asking confusing questions. These are questions that contain too much material for the participant to grasp at one time. By the time the whole question has been asked, the participant is confused. When faced with "double-barreled" questions, the participant is more concerned with which part to answer first than with critical thinking that offers ideas. Also, presenters sometimes offer unfamiliar vocabulary words or ideas that are above the participant's heads. This leads to frustration among students.

Cheek (1989) suggests that the presenter not ask participants questions that he or she knows the participants cannot answer. He further notes that everyone should be given a chance to participate and that a few participants' dominating the class should be avoided.

Advantages, Disadvantages, and Limitations of Questioning

When using the questioning instructional strategy, the presenter should be aware of the following advantages, disadvantages, and limitations.

Advantages of Questioning

1. It stimulates participant motivation and participation because it involves all participants.
2. It focuses participant attention and develops curiosity.
3. Participants can practice self-expression and gain pride in individual opinion.
4. It adds variety to the lesson.
5. Logically sequenced questions help reasoning skills.
6. It reveals individual abilities and interests that enhance the lesson.
7. It can be used to introduce, summarize, review, and clarify.
8. It emphasizes using ideas instead of just memorizing them.
9. It helps participants develop new insights and critical thinking.

Disadvantages of Questioning

1. Shy participants are reluctant to participate.
2. A small group of participants may take over the discussion.
3. Other participants may tune out while the presenter is with an individual participant.
4. If a participant's response is "shot down" by the presenter, the participant may become discouraged and withdraw.
5. Questions may not be phrased in ways that promote critical thinking and interest on the part of the participant.

Limitations of Questioning

1. Questions directed at large groups, as well as participants' responses to the question, are sometimes hard to hear.
2. It requires a large amount of class time because of the level of participant involvement.
3. The teacher must provide an open, noncritical environment that welcomes all responses.
4. Too much time is spent on questions that demand only lower-level thinking.
5. Overuse leads to predictability and boredom.

Examples or Applications

Questioning strategies should be chosen that appropriately target the level of participants, atmosphere of discussion, and depth of the subject matter. Narrow questions are used for factual drilling, whereas broad questions explore topics in greater depth. A good mix of both, beginning with narrow questions, can lead to a varied lesson that avoids boredom.

An effective approach to asking questions is to call on willing and nonwilling volunteers equally to provide each participant with the opportunity to share his or her thoughts. This encourages participation and confidence about opinions.

To improve participant responses that are weak, use questioning strategies that prompt the participant to correct, clarify, or expound on his or her answer. Begin with narrow questions that orient the participants with information that is familiar to them and then build as they redevelop their answers. Other participants should be encouraged to help struggling students with suggestions on improving their answers. This will not only involve the others but also take the "spotlight" off the individual participant.

Questioning strategies differ from presenter to presenter, depending on the unique situation. The presenter must adapt the appropriate questioning strategy to his or her participants. Hogg and Wilen (1976) state that if presenters incorporate self-analysis and participant analysis as beneficial feedback when evaluating their questioning style, then students learn more effectively. Question-asking strategies are only successful if they help the presenter achieve objectives and the participants master learning.

Summary

Whether narrow or broad, questioning sparks intellect and thought patterns when applied to meaningful subject matter. It provides the presenter with an awareness of participant comprehension of material and the participants with ways of presenting their ideas. When used effectively, it can enhance a lesson and promote interpersonal skills, understanding, and new avenues of thought.

References

Arnold, D., Atwood, R., & Rogers, V. (1973). An investigation of relationships among question level, response level and lapse time. *School Science and Mathematics, 7*(3), 591-594.

Buttery, T., & Michalak, D. (1978). Modifying questioning behavior via the teaching clinic process. *Educational Research Quarterly, 3*(2), 46-56.

Cheek, G. (1989). *Basic ideas for electrical instructors.* National Joint Apprenticeship and Training Committee for the Electrical Industry, Washington, DC.

Hogg, J., & Wilen, W. (1976). Evaluating teacher's questions: A new dimension in students' assessment of instruction. *Phi Delta Kappan, 58,* 281-282.

Houston, V. (1983). Improving the quality of classroom questions and questioning. *Educational Administration and Supervision, 24,* 17-28.

Sampson, G., Strykowski, B., Weinstein, T., & Walberg, H. (1987). The effects of teacher questioning levels on student achievement: A quantitative synthesis. *Journal of Educational Research, 80,* 290-295.

The Questioning Planning Sheet

Date:_____ Time:_____ Site:_____

Topic Statement:

Purpose of Questioning Session:

Directions for Participants:

Methods of Evaluating/Recording Participants' Responses:

     1.
     2.
     3.

Types of Questions to Be Used:

     1.
     2.
     3.

List of Questions:

Summary Notes:

The Questioning Evaluation Sheet

(🍎You may wish to have someone else consider these items,
as well as evaluating yourself.)

How appropriate were the questions for the participants? (level
of difficulty)

Did some of the questions require critical thinking?
___Yes ___No (Explain)

Were all participants adequately involved?
___Yes ___No (Explain)

🍎What reinforcements were used to reward for appropriate
responses?

How effectively did the classroom practitioner redirect participants when responses were inadequate?

🍎How well did the session accomplish the stated purpose?

🍎What was the facilitator's level of enthusiasm?

What was the general level of interest among participants?

🍎Did the summary serve to clarify any misunderstandings?

🍎Did the summary effectively bring closure to the session?

🍎What was best about this session?

🍎Suggestions for improvement: